THE DAO
FINAL

AN ADAPTATION OF THE *DAO DE JING*
DESIGNED TO SERVE THOSE FACING APOCALYPTIC TIMES

Adapted From Laozi's Original Text
BY SHUNYAMURTI

The Dao of the Final Days
An Adaptation of the *Dao De Jing*
Designed to Serve Those Facing Apocalyptic Times

Adapted From Laozi's Original Text
By Shunyamurti

Cover Art by Ajata
Format and Layout by Parvati
Copy Editing by Vajra

Sat Yoga
Pérez Zeledón, Costa Rica
+(506) 2100-7777
www.satyoga.org

Copyright © 2022 Sat Yoga Institute

No part of this publication may be reproduced, stored in or introduced into a retrieval system, or transmitted, in any forms or any means (electronic, mechanical, photocopying, recording or otherwise) without the prior written permission of the copyright owner of this book, except in the case of brief quotations embodied in critical articles or reviews. For permissions, please email: info@satyoga.org.

*This book is dedicated to the
Supreme Self, and to all those
Immortal Sages who have shown us
the Way*

Contents

Introduction — 1

Songs of the *Dao*

Song 1
The Way to Salvation — 14

Song 2
Beauty's Little Catch — 18

Song 3
Perceive the Blessing — 21

Song 4
Power Cut — 23

Song 5
The Noosphere — 25

Song 6
Dark Goddess — 27

Song 7
The Pinnacle of Grace — 29

SONG 8
ELEMENTAL KNOWLEDGE   31

SONG 9
REMOTE CONTROL   36

SONG 10
THE DAO ARRANGES ALL   37

SONG 11
THE VALUE OF EMPTINESS   38

SONG 12
BE INDESTRUCTIBLE   40

SONG 13
THE JOY OF INDIFFERENCE   41

SONG 14
THE REAL   42

SONG 15
BECOMING IMPERCEPTIBLE   44

SONG 16
THE ORIGIN AND DESTINY OF BEING   47

SONG 17
THE TRAJECTORY OF CULTURE   50

SONG 18
ANY DAY NOW   52

SONG 19
GNOSIS   54

SONG 20
BE READY   56

SONG 21
THE ORDEAL   58

SONG 22
TRUE DEVOTION   60

SONG 23
THE KNOCKOUT   63

SONG 24
THE DAO IS STRICT   66

SONG 25
NO MYSTERY   68

SONG 26
THE FINISH   71

SONG 27
PERFECT VISION   73

Song 28
The Wedding Feast   75

Song 29
Be Unattached   78

Song 30
Trust   81

Song 31
The Only Nuisance   84

Song 32
Functions of the Dao   86

Song 33
Love for the Real   90

Song 34
The Test   91

Song 35
Real Market Value   93

Song 36
The Hidden Power   95

Song 37
Redemption   98

SONG 38
TRUE VIRTUE   100

SONG 39
THE ARRIVAL   103

SONG 40
THE DANCE HALL   108

SONG 41
THE PERFECT INSTRUMENT   110

SONG 42
THE GRAND DIALECTIC   112

SONG 43
THE CHAINS WILL BREAK   116

SONG 44
CALIBRATE YOUR COMPASS   118

SONG 45
THE POWER TO GOVERN   120

SONG 46
EXODUS   121

SONG 47
INWARD JOURNEY   123

Song 48
The Phoenix   125

Song 49
Why Sages Laugh   127

Song 50
Rite of Passage   129

Song 51
The Mark of the Blessed   131

Song 52
When All is Lost   133

Song 53
The Crown   135

Song 54
Mastering Serenity   137

Song 55
The Sublime Innocence of Sages   139

Song 56
The Adorable Real   141

Song 57
Decision Time   144

SONG 58
THE NEW ORDER   146

SONG 59
THE REAL ECONOMY   148

SONG 60
THE FINAL SOLUTION   151

SONG 61
THE LAST DAYS   154

SONG 62
ONE SELF   156

SONG 63
THE MIND OF A SAGE   157

SONG 64
EXISTENCE AND BEING   159

SONG 65
THE WINNING STRATEGY   161

SONG 66
GET THE DRIFT   164

SONG 67
WHAT BODHISATTVAS KNOW   166

SONG 68
BRINGERS OF PEACE   168

SONG 69
THE TURNING TIDE   169

SONG 70
YOU MUST AWAKEN   172

SONG 71
THE CURE   174

SONG 72
THE ANSWER   177

SONG 73
THE COST IS HIGH   179

SONG 74
DON'T SELL YOUR SOUL   181

SONG 75
THEIR BIG MISTAKE   183

SONG 76
THE WISEST COURSE   185

SONG 77
THE DAO OF ARCHERY   188

Song 78
The Ultimate Game   190

Song 79
The Reward   193

Song 80
A New Mandate of Heaven   195

Song 81
Beyond Temptation   197

Epilogue   199

A Final Note on Virtue   213

Glossary   217

INTRODUCTION

The *Dao De Jing*—The Book of the Way and Its Virtue—is a timeless masterpiece of wisdom. But to serve the souls of these last days before the final collapse of planetary civilization, the profound wisdom of Laozi required an update to be properly understood and assimilated by postmodern minds. Only small changes were required to orient the principles of Truth to apply to our current situation. Laozi's greatness in channeling the Way is that it makes clear even now, thousands of years later, the way to channel Dao anew. It is our responsibility to ferment the old wine and re-bottle it for the refreshment of all who are on the hero's journey.

Keep in mind as you read, that for the ancient sages, the concept of Virtue also meant real power. Those who are attuned to the Way not only increase their serenity and intelligence, but simultaneously their compassionate goodness and their power to endure, uplift, and creatively effect benevolent change. Our hope is to transmit without flaws the great sage Laozi's deep understanding of the immortals' path and apply those principles to the task of commanding the forces in the matrix now in play.

Although the word Dao can generally be translated as Way, in this adaptation it is most often being left in its original Chinese form. This is because this central term also has other significations and implications that cannot all be combined in a single word. Dao refers to the vibrational frequency of the Supreme Intelligence manifesting as the Universe. Dao also refers to the paradoxical strategies and tactics that a sage will apply in particular situations of difficulty. Dao can further refer to the state of consciousness of the illumined sage, including the realization of absolute nonduality, the interconnectedness of every being, every seemingly separate thing, and every event in this holographic simulation. In that sense, Dao is equivalent to the Vedic term for Ultimate Reality, Brahman. That makes it equally equivalent to the later Mahayana concept of Buddha Nature. And of course, Dao can also be considered the Will of God.

The word Dao derives from the Sanskrit term Dharma, the core concept of the ancient yogis of the lost era of Bharata that signifies both the accurate way to act in the world in order to produce the optimal karmic outcome, as well as the attainment of Infinite Mind. Dao can also signify the power of a sage to employ the mind in supernormal modes in accord with the Supreme Will. The Sanskrit term for this power is *siddhi**, and one who has mastered that level of consciousness is a *siddha*.

To abide in the Dao means to live in the highest level of consciousness, in resonance with the Source of universal Being. In that sense, the Dao is equivalent to *Atman*, the yogic term for the Real Self. This is also known as our true nature, our essence, which is formless and therefore capable of shapeshifting on the phenomenal plane. The Kashmir Shaivite sages of India referred to this ultimate Real as *Chaitanya*, and its creative power as *Spanda*.

The understanding of the Dao was elaborated in a unique and original way by Laozi, which was developed further by the contemporary sage Zhuangzi, whose ideas are also incorporated in this adaptation. But we can perceive the same wisdom in the innermost teachings of all the great spiritual traditions of the world. Abraham, Moses, and the early prophets of Israel, especially the Essenes and

---

**All italicized Sanskrit, Chinese, and Latin terms are defined in the glossary that follows the text, unless they are defined in the text itself.*

Enochians, were attuning to the Dao. The Dao was clearly taught by Jesus Christ, although the Church later banned and burned most of the authentic gospels. The Dao can be recognized in the Holy Quran and many Sufi texts. Numerous sages in recent world history have manifested the Dao. But today, in these dark times of dumbed-down materialistic culture and corrupted religious lineages, the Dao is nearly extinct. But since the Dao is our nature, it cannot really be lost. We have the capacity to attune to the Dao if we are willing to train our minds to sustain perfect stillness, purify our hearts to a state of unconditional love, empathy, courage, nobility, and joy, and surrender our wills and all personal desire to the Supreme Presence.

If we attempt to understand the cosmos from the perspective of the ego, using differentiating analytic logic, it will appear infinitely complex and indeterminate. But from the level of the Supreme Intelligence, the universe is absolutely simple and immediate. This is because at the level at which the Dao functions, the world is not other than the One Self. Moreover, at the highest level of consciousness, both space and time are recognized as illusory. The entire implicate order of cosmic evolution is here now, to those who have the Eye of Dao with which to see. This is also famously known by such terms as the Eye of Ra by the ancient Egyptian sages, and the Eye of Shiva by Indian yogis, or simply as the Third Eye. To attain the Dao, we must open our Third Eye.

To open the Third Eye, however, we must attune to the Dao. This can seem to be the ultimate catch-22, an impossibility to attain. But if we look deeper, without the burden of ordinary logic, and recognize that the Dao is always already present as our true nature, then we can understand that our Third Eye is open even now, and we must simply start looking through it, rather than only focusing through the two worldly eyes that see only illusions, projections, impermanent appearances, and cannot perceive that all these are governed by a higher power.

Simply attune to the Dao and you will be guided safely through this time of tribulations. The only caveat is that you must be willing and able to drop your preconceptions, your current belief systems, and your conventional ideas of good and evil. You must understand and palpably feel that death is not the end, that there is nothing to fear, and that all beings die, but only on the physical level. All planets also die. The universe itself undergoes birth and death.

Once we recognize that we are at the point of planetary death—and even cosmic obliteration—and we have refined our intellects to the realization of eternity, we will feel what a blessing this is for our simulated world of suffering beings. We can also then navigate calmly through the current moment of barely disguised global genocide via bioweaponry and other high-tech means of destruction and enslavement of the human race. But what is of essential importance is that we should not judge this event through the eyes of conventional morality and fall into rage or despair. That is the great trap that we must avoid.

By attuning to the Dao, we can then see this whole panorama with the Eye of Shiva, the ultimate destroyer of worlds, who acts when those worlds have become evil. This world of cruel and oppressive dictators will come to an end, and soon, by virtue of the Dao. The Will of Shiva is absolutely benevolent, and this world will be painlessly sucked into the Singularity—an infinitesimal and infinitely dense point of infinite power, intelligence, and awareness. This point of eternal light is equivalent to the theistic concept of the Godhead, or Supreme Self. This point of absolute power can be palpated by the inwardly directed attention at any moment, and is the basis of what yogis call *samadhi*. To be in *sahaja samadhi*, the yogic term for perpetual abidance in the Supreme Reality, is to be attuned to the Dao.

Once one accepts that the current episode of seemingly unprecedented malignant murder of all life on our planet is a natural cyclic occurrence, inevitable and necessary, and in accordance with God's will, we can relax our resistance and focus on the higher meaning and implications of this event. First, we can recognize that all that is happening is symptomatic of the terminal illness of Nature on planet Earth, and that this was caused by the fall of humanity into demonic depravity, having had our souls captured and usurped by the thought-form we call the ego.

The ego is a fabricated operating system, not an authentic self. But once the soul manufactured the ego to function as a buffer and an instrument of control, the Frankenstein monster of egocentricity gradually took over both the individual and the collective consciousness. The ego ripped us away from Nature, replicating itself in every newborn baby, until the ego parasite became globalized. The ego then replicated itself digitally, eventually producing machines with artificial intelligence, culminating in quantum computers capable of housing the ego more effectively than could be achieved by the human brain. So now, the original monster has created another even more powerful terminator version of itself, which has launched its blitzkrieg against an unsuspecting human species no longer needed as its host.

Against this inhuman opponent of immense computational power, do humans have a chance? Is there any weapon at our disposal that could overthrow the tyrannical, soulless beast that is taking over our world? Is there any relevance to studying the Dao? Indeed, we are in the ultimate David vs. Goliath moment of Truth. In fact, there will need to be many Davids, because we face many Goliaths. So please keep your spiritual slingshot handy and keep improving your aim. Despite appearances, it is wise to place your bet on the victory of those who wield the Dao.

We are in a war, and we must master the principles of seventh-generation warfare. We must not gauge our vision of what is happening based on a terrestrial frame of reference. The battlefield is interdimensional. Even though the enemy controls the phenomenal space, the high ground of transcendental consciousness is not accessible to it. There are dark forces in the astral planes as well, which the ancient gnostics called the archons, but beyond the jurisdiction of the demiurge lies the realm of the divine powers. We should not forget to factor in to our strategic considerations—nor fail to form alliances with—such principalities as the angels and archangels, the *devas*, buddhas, and ascended *mahasiddhas*. But to claim the high ground known by such appellations as *Nirvana*, *Akanishta*, and *Paramdhama*, we must be fully in resonance with the highest godly angels. We must have purified our consciousness to an impeccable degree of perfection. The skill to wield the potencies of the Dao depends on our self-discipline and renunciation of material attachments.

Other than a few ultra-religious Christians, very few people today believe in the possibility of what the Book of Revelations refers to as the Rapture. Nor would most people be interested in being raptured up into the clouds of unknowing. To them, it would seem indistinguishable from death. But the Rapture refers to a state of Being that could be called the Death of Death. It has nothing to do with the disappearance of one's mortal body, but rather the ascension of consciousness to the realm of the Absolute. In that sense, the Dao is the portal to the Rapture. The Dao offers freedom beyond capture by the ego. Until we have been raptured—the Vedantic yogis call that state *Sat Chit Ananda*—we cannot know the implications of being gifted with the grace of freedom of consciousness to know and deploy its total potential.

The Dao is our original nature, prior to incarnation in these fragile human bodies. By virtue of the Dao, we can sustain continuity of consciousness throughout the process of cosmic destruction and a new emission of a cosmic simulation that will be free of evil forces—a Kingdom of Heaven—a paradise for all who live there. The creation and repopulation of a new world is the way that is destined to gain victory in the current contest between the divine and demonic polarities of the Real.

The Dao is above all worldly jurisdictions, cannot be subjected to any mandates of a tyrant, nor can the power of the Dao be limited by any decrees of a human legislature. You have the divine birthright as an offspring of God to claim your divine right of kings. Surrender to the Dao alone brings the promise of triumph. It must be a complete triumph over death, illusion, fear, egocentricity, and the energy of consciousness itself. This is no small matter. That is why there are so few authentic sages. But there is no reason you cannot be one of them. We are all created equal as souls, regardless of the anatomy, physical condition, or skin tone of our physical vehicles, and we all have free will. But we must give this task our undistracted attention. To attune to the Dao requires wholehearted dedication, accurate knowledge, and love of truth, goodness, and beauty.

To attune to the Dao is both simple and extremely difficult. It is simple because the Dao is your natural state. But it is impossible for the unnatural ego to reach it. You must extract your soul from the ego in order to attune to the Dao. The Dao will then take you to the Supreme One. The recommended way of extracting your soul from ego domination is to both recognize your divine nature and open your heart in total devotion to God (or Buddha Nature, etc.). You must keep your attention willfully focused on the inmost Self, the unmoving Center of Consciousness, until that state of silent, still presence becomes natural again.

You will soon find that you are empty, in fact, you are Emptiness itself, the Void, Absolute Nothingness. No thoughts—especially no I-thought—or emotions will remain. There will be no projections. What had been perceived as a world will be recognized as the internal functioning of the One Self, the Supreme Intelligence, which is Nothing—nothing actual, but infinite potentiality that also dreams into existence the unreal temporal actuality. The mode of consciousness will shift from subject-object duality to nonduality. The illusion of a separate world will be overcome. The Dream and the Dreamer are one. The Dao thus spontaneously functions in unity with the Whole. The joyous laughter of complete understanding and reunification with the Godhead is the grand prize that awaits you when you embody the Great Dao and Its mighty Virtue.

Behold the Dao!

Songs of the *Dao* of the Final Days

Song 1

The Way to Salvation

The Dao is the Way to Liberation
From the matrix of illusion
Known as the world

But the Way cannot be grasped
From an egocentric mindset
Only from Emptiness
That saturates each frame of being-time

The Dao that can be reduced
To a name or concept
That could be grasped by a created entity
Is not the authentic Dao

The Dao is Real
But its locus is a dimension above that of thought
Not an idea that can be contained in thought
Since it belongs to the Unknowable Thinker
The Mind that is dreaming the world

The Dao programs all the algorithms
That produce every appearance
And mental object and event

To pierce the veil
That separates you from the Dao
Be without intention
Totally empty
Totally present
Stretched to the limits of perception
And open to what enters from Beyond

To see the beauty of the world
Realize that the intelligence and love
Of the Supreme One permeates each moment
And all beings and appearances
And the consciousness to whom it all appears

Even in this time of ugliness
Of the horror of planetary death
Beauty is everywhere
And ecstasy is our natural state

The Dao and the world's unfoldment
Are not two

Open your Third Eye and see
With nondual vision

The Dao is timeless
While the world is ephemeral
The Dao will continue
Long after this world's demise
But even the momentary is eternal
And death has no effect on the Real

The Dao has been called by many names
Including God
Nothingness
The Self of the Universe
The Absolute

The true meaning of those terms
Cannot be understood
By a mind that is split internally
Between subject and object
And imagines itself bound by karma

Silent focus on the Infinite Self
Until immersion is complete
Will bring the rapture of salvation

Even when it seems all hope is lost
In this hall of mirrors
That is the cosmic holographic simulation
The immeasurable creative potency
Of the Dao
Is undiminished

The grace of the Dao
Even now
Is fully present
In the center of your mind

Song 2

Beauty's Little Catch

When the desire for beauty enters the world
It means real beauty has been lost
Ugly beings will appear
Often glamorous and seductive in form
But selfish and narcissistic
Because desire is a projection of lack

Since the world is your dream
Time will bring your character its complement
Which the Self perceives as symmetry

No appearance remains constant
As the character either entropically devolves
And its world becomes increasingly grotesque
Or the soul returns to the radiance of the Source
And its world becomes a heaven

When your world has turned monstrous and vile
Return to your Supreme Self
Shine with the perfect beauty of goodness

Be cleansed of desire and fear
Transmit love that is free of judgment
And Truth that empowers all hearts

Awaken your miraculous powers
To redream the world in the image of God

Abide in the stillness of the Self
The Dao will do the work
Of arranging Destiny
To mirror your purity of heart

Everyone's projections are different
What is bad for one is good for another
What is difficult for one is easy for the other

All projections arise from a sense of lack
Which is only ignorance of one's true nature
Which has no lack

The Dao will lead you to the Source
Take the path to Emptiness
Endure the death of ego
And discover the Fullness beyond
That is always here and now
The awesome Intelligence

And timeless Bliss that is the Self

The state of the world should not concern you
Let the processes of decay and planetary death
Do their sacred work without any interference
Accept with neither sorrow nor dismay
The massive euthanasia underway

Annihilation is always followed by new life
Trust the Dao

Be courageous
Truthful and loyal
To love that conquers death

Uphold the principles of Dharma
Non-violence
Generosity
Compassion

And celebrate eternal Life

Song 3

Perceive the Blessing

When people were free from envy and greed
Psychopaths could not rule
But now they have taken over
Acting with impunity to enslave and exterminate
The masses who naively follow orders
Believing false promises
Of health and a return to normal life

A sage will find a community
Or found one
Far from the maddened crowds
Where wisdom prevails
And the Dao is honored

If ego death is required to join
And activities are joyous
If success is not measured by quantity
Of possessions or profit
Then neither theft nor violence will intrude

Return with a silent mind
To the Eternal Sun within
Detach from phenomena
And the ersatz world will end

This is the Dao of the final days
When the Angel of Death arrives
And the Singularity begins to shine
Through the entire simulation

Do not be concerned with physical survival
The immortal Self is not affected
By the body's death
And the end of this sick world
Is a blessing

Song 4
Power Cut

The Dao leads souls to Emptiness
A sage who is empty of ego
Is filled with the power of Truth

When the Dao presides
In a culture
The people are simple and honest
Peaceful and content

When the Dao is obscured
And the world is empty of sages
Evil forces emerge

When society is ruled by demons
Enacting their perverted desires
The Dao will not allow life to go on

The hologram will have its power cut
And Mind will disappear into the Void
Until the next Creation

To know the Dao
Cease producing thought and emotion
Become aware of the radiance within
And recognize the world is only That

Learn to see with the divine eye
The beauty of the Source
And know that God is here right now

Song 5

The Noosphere

Heaven and Earth are heartless
We creatures are nothing but straw dogs
To be destroyed once our karma is complete

The sage is equally indifferent

The world is impermanent
A simulation lacking essence
Yet a cinematic masterpiece
Of awesome allure

The Dao pumps out worlds
Like a bellows
And sucks them into Nothingness again

But the imaginal space
Between Heaven and Earth
The magical symbolic dimension
Is given to be mastered by our mind

The noosphere is pervaded
By information waves

Decode them
And you have real power

But be clear that it is better
To develop what you have within
Than to download a great deal of data
That goes nowhere

And leaves you in the matrix
As before

Song 6

Dark Goddess

The Life Force
That animates the Dream Field
Never dies
She is the energy of becoming
The Dark Goddess

This unknowable immortal
Feminine Power
Is the Mother of the world

Wispy and delicate
An apparition of delight
She only seems to be with you
But for a true encounter
You must reach Her Lotus Throne

There is a way to earn Her favor

Her power to create and to destroy
Is limitless

She cannot be possessed
But She will surrender to your love
If you are a true and pure
And noble knight

And if you are a woman
She may choose to fill your form
When She wants to be embodied
To bring the grace of Heaven
To the Earth

Song 7

The Pinnacle of Grace

The lifespan of the world
Is nearly over
Matter will soon return to Light

Sages have already merged their minds
With the Transcendental Sun

The unified field
Containing the entire cosmos
Will be sucked into the Singularity
Only the Zero Point will prevail

Withdraw attention into the Heart
Where only the Self abides
And prepare to awaken
From the cosmic dream

The Dream will begin again
And long-lost archetypal forms
Will reappear in glory

As the gods return
To play in another Golden Age

Now is the time to be present
Let go of will and thought
Return to Pure Awareness

All the mysteries will be revealed
And all the hidden powers
Of consciousness will be unveiled

But first die to the I
Drop every why
That is the grace of Liberation

Song 8

Elemental Knowledge

Mastery of all the elements
And powers of perception
Is a requirement
For those determined to obtain
The key to the power of the Dao

Be on the Earth but do not take birth
Remain as Uncreated Presence
You are the formless Abyss
The Emptiness of Absolute Mind

Disengage from the elements
To wield their potent magic

Learn what the world is really made of
See through the surface to the inner core
The elements are so much more
And yet are just a metaphor

Some say the highest element is Water

Know how to flow
Around all obstacles
Dive beneath the dams
Be able to evaporate
And levitate as cloud

Rest in sacred mountains as the mist
Precipitate as morning dew
Offering the liquidity of life

Be the Air that all must breathe
Suffused with subtle light
The unbound Wind of Spirit
Inspire
Empower
Overturn imprisoning beliefs
Roar in perfect freedom
Create an atmosphere
Of love and celebration
Available for all to inhale

Be the Fire
That burns away impurity
Incinerate illusion
Consume all suffering
Reduce to ashes all remorse

Be the Fire
That annihilates all fear
The sacred flame
That lights our way through time

Be the Sacrificial Fire
In which all images and idols are destroyed
Set all limited identities ablaze

Be the Funeral Pyre
Cremating all desire
Bursting with intensity
That delivers life from death

Be the Signal Fire
Transmitting the message
That the Lord has come
To redeem the world

Do not forget the element of Ether
The Field in which all space and time arise
The Ether is the extreme unction
That pops the quantum wave function
Returning the cosmos
To the formless Void
And provides the raw material

For future worlds

But the most important of the five elements
That can be sensed
Is Earth
The lowliest
The one we walk on
The Ground of Being

Be the Earth
As the majesty of mountains
Solid
Unmoving
And still

Be the Earth
Capable of erupting with fire
A volcano of immeasurable power

Be the Earth
Always ready to shake the creatures
With a tremor or a massive shock

But mostly be the Earth
That produces fruits and flowers
And vegetables that support all forms of life

And give all space to roam

One more element remains to be attained
The *Shiva Tattva*
The control room for the Game
The element of Intelligence Itself
Supremely pure and accurate
Where every destiny is ordained

To some this element is known
As the Philosopher's Stone
But many sages concur
The true name is Excalibur

The Sword of Truth
Waiting for the rightful king
To draw it from the stone

You are called to make the journey
Deep into the Godhead
To claim the authority
To rule in the Kingdom of Heaven

We are contestants
In the real Olympic Games
Practice the Dao to perfection

Song 9

Remote Control

Sages minimize their wants
Abide in inner solitude
And silence

Empty and detached
They let time's pendulum swing
Without resistance

Conditions oscillate
Sages are not troubled by loss

They steer the ship
By remote control
And span the ocean as a whole

When their worldly task is complete
They gladly take a back seat
The deeper mission
Must be finished from there

Song 10

The Dao Arranges All

The sages have given clear instructions

Unify *Yin* and *Yang*
Love and Law
Samsara and *Nirvana*
The knower and the known

Stop all thoughts
Slow the breath
Abide as Empty Presence

The splendor of the Real will be revealed
Let the Dao arrange the new world order

Song 11

The Value of Emptiness

The spokes are many
The wheel is one
The hub is the Zero Point

Without the emptiness
In the center
Neither the one nor the many
Will function

Globs of clay can be made into a pot
The empty space in the middle
Is what makes it beneficial

A room is only vacant expanse
Bounded by its walls
Doorways and windows must be cut out
Without the empty space
A house would have no worth

We are useful only when
Our Emptiness within
Is preserved

Song 12

Be Indestructible

Those who are driven by lust
For sensual stimulation
Become stupid

Dispassion brings wisdom
Wisdom brings dispassion

Watching violence makes one vicious
Objectifying others makes one abject

Possessiveness feeds one's angst

Fear of loss of power
Means it is already lost

Return to silence
Be Empty as the Void

That is the Source of power
That cannot be destroyed

Song 13

The Joy of Indifference

Whether you are praised or slandered
Must not matter
Having any ego is a flaw

Immunity to false projections
Is a sign of psychic health

Indifference to the envy of others
Is imperative
To fulfill your sacred task

To realize that there is no world
Beyond the Self

Song 14

The Real

The Real cannot be seen with the eyes
It is formless
It cannot be heard with the ears
The Real is soundless
You cannot catch it with your hands
Or even your mind
The Real is nothing
But your Self

The Self is Absolute Nothingness
Yet the Self alone
Projects and contains the whole world
And is our ultimate abode
The Self is the only God

The Self alone is Real
And shows the Way to Liberation
From this matrix of illusion

Thus the wise do not fear death

Nor the world's approaching end
By following the Dao
The heart stays safe

The Self that cannot be grasped
Will always hold you

Surrender and God's love
Will enfold you

Empty your mind and open your heart
To be filled with the Self's light and love
The virtue of the Dao is Real

Song 15

Becoming Imperceptible

The ancient sages embodied the Dao
The medieval Daoists understood it

Today it is only a word

Attunement to the Dao is blocked
By mental chatter and emotion
The ego cannot function
As a vessel of the Dao

To know the Dao requires total presence

The sages of the ancient world
Lived in such deep *samadhi*
They were inscrutable
To those with shallow minds

This is how their students
Described their demeanor

Cautious and measured
As though crossing a winter stream
Covered with thin ice

Quiet and reserved
As if not wanting to disturb any neighbors

Respectful and dignified
Attentive to the other
As if an honored guest of royalty

Flowing and yielding
Shapeshifting and gleaming
Like icicles thawing
Into sparkling drops of water

Simple and solid
As a block of wood

Vast and open
Like a broad river valley

The sages served as catalysts
For troubled souls whose wounds
Required ego death to heal

In their presence
Defiled beings felt like muddy water
Finally becoming clear
The dirt filtered out
By the purifying energy
Of unconditional acceptance

Those who value the Dao
Are indeterminate and free
Without judgment

Imperceptible
Yet shining brazenly
In splendor
Only the true seekers can see

SONG 16

THE ORIGIN AND DESTINY OF BEING

The Dao is potent without limits
Yet seemingly passive and still
The Dao is Real
Beyond Being or becoming

The sage's heart is always still
Even when the mind and body move
And there is always fascination
For the wonders produced by the Dao

Aham aham
I am I
The final mantra of a Vedic sage
Is utterly equivalent
To the word of the sage of the Dao

Wuwu
No nothing
No reification or commentary
No concepts or objects or thoughts

Realize stillness as the Self
Containing all that happens
As nothing

No one acts
But all unfolds in perfection

Ceaseless change
That appears in timeless Mind

Stillness
The origin and destiny
Of Being

After every cycle of time
The universe of matter collides
With its twin of antimatter
Annihilating both

The Void that awaits
In the background
Of your mind
Has been there since before the world
And soon will swallow time and space

What you were

Before the beginning
Will be revealed at the climax
Of our cosmic play

The Light that will flash in the final instant
Brighter than a thousand suns
Shines in the core of your Being
Waiting to explode
When your ego dies into the Source

In these final days
Of planetary slaughter
Before the Omega Point arrives
Do not allow the chaos
In the fading simulation
To obscure the glory of the Real

Song 17

The Trajectory of Culture

When a culture is young and still inspired
By the ideals of the founders
The people creatively develop their arts

They live out great adventures
While most are barely aware
Of the governmental officers
Who work behind the scenes

When culture has attained success and comfort
Then the leader is loved and highly praised

In the following period of slow decline
Rulers arise who are hated and feared

And in the end
When the civilization
Is approaching its death
Rulers appear who are idiots despised by all

When coherence and truthfulness disappear
Corruption and incompetence grow unchecked

A leader who is wise will not use force
Nor make promises that cannot be kept

When projects work out well
Credit is given to God
And the virtue of the Dao

Song 18

Any Day Now

When the Dao is abandoned by the people
Kindness and justice rise in value

When those virtues have degraded
They are replaced by the discourse of reason
Which soon devolves
Into the facile ideology of pseudo-scientism

Hypnotized by technological wonders
The masses of people are deceived
Their education is dumbed down
And they are slowly turned into fools
Who accept their own enslavement
So long as it is called protection

When foul play is the method of the rulers
And traitors take control of the thrones
They demand strict obedience from all
Especially when they order
The entire population

To commit suicide

You can hear the mountains call
It is time to slip away

The system will fall
Any day

Song 19

Gnosis

Don't be impressed
By displays of wide knowledge or talent
But only by virtue and joy

Don't get entangled in debate
Serenity and silence
Comprise the Way

Don't be disturbed
By cunning false friends
Or profit-seeking would-be helpers
Don't be naïve about theft or fraud

This whole world is a fraud
We have been stolen from God
By our own cunning minds
And profit-seeking

The Dao is beyond hope and fear
And not concerned with judgment

But always staying clear
The sage is undaunted
In the night of the living dead
Nor will awakened souls
Be shocked to see
The Supreme Sun shine
When midnight strikes the world

Even in an ashram's calm
Egos will fall into psychosis

The only cure is gnosis

Song 20

Be Ready

Be ever ready to respond
To the unexpected

In stillness that cannot be disturbed

Fulfill your duties
Speak gentle words
Combining Law with Love
See only the One in all

Be ceaselessly prepared to die
But don't be stupid

Don't care if others think you're mad
But drop immature inclinations

Solitude is best
Even in community
Be empty and alone

Wander on trails where birds are singing
And fragrant wildflowers bloom

Though people are terrified of dying
Nature does not fear doom
Adhere to the Dao and feel no gloom

Song 21

The Ordeal

All of our creativity
Intelligence
And strength of will
Are siphoned from the reservoir of Dao

Those locked in ego's shell
Cannot perceive the Dao's brilliant virtue

Yet the Dao sends hints
And light that can be glimpsed
And delivers insights that shock one's heart

The act of taking refuge in the Self
In total surrender
Dropping narratives
Projections and beliefs
Being penetrated to the core
Is enough to end all grief

But first you must pass through despair

And the terror of being vulnerable again
And feel the tragic lack of essence and power
Without dissociation
Or diffusion
Or somatization
Or another defense

Surrender completely
In abject Emptiness
And wait
To be filled with the Pillar of Light

Ego's annihilation brings dread
To an end
It can be gradual or quick

This rite of passage
Is an easier ordeal
For those who love
The Real

Song 22

True Devotion

Bow to the Dao
By standing for Truth

Kiss the feet of the Lord
Who is dancing on your head
By igniting your crown chakra

Listen from the Heart
And the lies of the mind will die

Prostration is the basis of religion
Be humble
Be nothing
When silent and open
Your Heart will receive the Light

Devotion to the Real
Dilates the soul
Inviting God to enter

In the consummated union of love
Divine nectar flows
And Christ is born
In ego's manger

The Buddha is enlightened
Beneath the Bodhi Tree
Once all efforts and ideas have failed
And nothing remains but presence

At the root of arborescent mind
Lies the underground rhizome of the Real
That bequeaths the power to Be
The omnicentric unified field

The non-existent mirror
That the ego seeks to know itself
Is always free of dust
Because not even dust
Can find it

Realize you are no one
And there is no one but you

A single proposition is true

Wuwu

If this is understood
All is done

Song 23

The Knockout

Silence is the only truthful speech
Spoken words are a faulty translation

When talk is needed
Whisper and be brief

Storms do not last
And people hide from them
Stormy minds squander their strength

A tranquil voice reveals the Dao
When Presence has been realized in the Heart

Success and failure have no meaning
To the egoless mind

Life and death
Are not a concern

Virtue is the power that commands

But does not deign to differentiate
Between good and bad
Virtue knows only perfection

Although tyranny combined with technology
Is now destroying all that humans hold dear
The sage understands this is needed
To awaken their anesthetized hearts

Artificial intelligence
Cannot defeat the Real

Technology does only one thing well
It was made for the harrowing of Hell

A master artist does not seek fame
A great painting needs no frame

The Cosmic Dreamer needs no assistance
A new world is being dreamed without resistance

The wellspring of love
That brings the gift of death and redemption
Is your own cosmic nature being born

Despite one's surface stains

Underlying purity remains

All self-doubt
Should be knocked out

SONG 24

THE DAO IS STRICT

Stand tall
But not taller than you are

Know when to move fast
And when to be cautious and go slow

To brag is to lose credibility
But false modesty is also a flaw
Benign delight is the Way

The wise won't leave the Dao
For a few vain minutes of fame
Nor fall into the mud of karma
To indulge a rescue fantasy
Or a leftover need to be loved

Keep your Temple sacred and clean

Report only the amount of Truth

To which you have surrendered

The Dao is very strict
With its servants

Song 25
No Mystery

Before and beyond
The appearance of the world
And finite mind
The Great Void alone abides

A circular wave
Ripples out from the Center
Laying out the field
In which every cosmos is spawned

The Great Drama ensues
In toroidal time
On a moebius strip
In which immanence ends
As transcendence

The wave will soon withdraw again
Into the Zero Point from which it emerged

The Dao creates and sustains

And will destroy
This holographic matrix
We no longer enjoy

Because unmitigated evil now rules
And the pendulum swings ever faster
The ultimate Good must soon return

This earthly hell will be cut and spliced
To its beginning
When the world was birthed as a paradise

Salvation is return to the luminous Abyss
Annihilation is the test of our faith

Our greatness consists in our resolve
To obtain the Final Revelation
Which requires that our concepts dissolve

This is our Way
The wise all say
To break free from the matrix of duality

There is no need for a Way
Silence is already knowledge
All difference is more of the same

The shadow is only the sign of the Light
The world is no other than the Void

This Mystery was never concealed
Not even by an empty field

Song 26

The Finish

It is better to be heavy duty
Industrial strength
Rather than flimsy and weak

Stillness is the most effective action
Be both up and down at once
And be neither
Be done with allowing duality
To twirl you around
Its finger

Be fully equipped
Need nothing

In these final days
Of our simulated world
Which is only a finishing school
Don't be obsessed with physical survival

Disembark

From the character you play
Then refine it to express the highest Truth
And the purest Love
And the greatest Power

The Dao will exterminate the demons
Your only task
Is to merge into the Absolute Self

The bliss of pure and total Presence
Shines in your Sacred Heart

Now don't be late
To graduate
Be finished with concern for fate

Song 27

Perfect Vision

An expert hunter leaves no tracks
An adept speaker wastes no words
The Self directs but does not appear

A sage will not bother to resist
What does not intrinsically exist

This dying world will simply vanish
It will happen very soon
But don't expect to receive
Advance notice

The secret is not hidden
From those who want to know
And are willing to pay the price
For Liberation

The wise care not for life or reputation
But for grace

They neither rescue nor abandon anyone
There is no one to save
In this holographic cinematic
Solipsistic show
Except one's soul

To the ignorant ego
The sage seems blind
To the fiendish horror at large in the world
Knowing it to be unreal
But the sage is neither in denial nor naïve
The sage has taken leave
Of the entire phenomenal illusion

Once the ego bubble has been popped
There is no need for any further decision

With the Third Eye open
One enjoys perfect vision

Song 28

The Wedding Feast

Siddhas protect yoginis
From their own bestial nature
Honoring the feminine power
Of Beauty and Love

Shakti is revered by Shiva
And the feeling is mutual
They play at being two
But are forever One

Love is the unity
Of Wisdom and Beauty
Goodness emerges from Her womb
But so does Her second son
Power
Who desires Her love
But will not surrender

Samsara and *Nirvana*
Collude in a game of hide and seek

Possession and rejection
The beginning and the end

The unfoldment of the cosmic game
Of yes and no
And every mode of duality
Based on the semblance of separation
Ends with the revelation
That the seeker and the sought
Have always been the same
But staged
As Symmetry versus Complementarity
Performing a dual striptease
Of entanglement and indeterminacy

The final act
After crucifixion
And resurrection
And the Mother's grand ascent
To Her lotus throne in Heaven
Is the Immaculate Conception
Known as the Singularity
And then of course
The virgin birth of a divine new world

The honeymoon of Shiva and Shakti

That is happening right now
Is the good news
Of these last auspicious days

This most sacred Event is ordained
But rarely reported
Since it drives the demons crazy

They can hear the Lovers laughing
And they know the wedding party
Is only just beginning

But they will not be invited
To the Feast

SONG 29

BE UNATTACHED

Using brute force in fighting evil would fail
The ruling order feeds upon that fire

Stillness is the greatest shield
Emptiness the armor
And Divine Love is the weapon of the wise
But one must be mounted on the Tiger

Lord Shiva prefers to ride on a Bull
Since He has no predatory inclinations
And there are Goddesses who ride on Swans

For you
They have reserved the Elephant
If you have the courage to climb onboard

Be immovable
And massive as a mountain
Unafraid

Knowing the secret of Power

Connect all the nodes
In the entire morphic field
Contained in the Cosmic Self
The Field Marshal who deploys the Dao

The Dao governs all through coherence
In superposition
To the plane of appearance

Keep the mind in resonance
With the Supreme Intelligence
Indifferent to life and death

Presence is more subtle
Than particles and waves
Emanating divine vibrations
That induce synchronistic events

The sage learns to ignore
The body's hunger and pain
Never moving from the Center Point

Unattached to any situation

Or any sentient being or thing
Without concern for loss or gain

The wise accept and ordain

Song 30

Trust

Sustain your community
United with the Dao

Get fully dressed for action
First put on humility as underwear
Then slip on your T-shirt of wisdom
Your dress or pants of beauty and courage
Your socks of compassion
And the shoes of skillful means
Don't forget to add the purity of gloves
And finally put on the hat of sovereign power

The warrior of the Dao
Is not aggressive
Use of force or coercion brings blowback
One must wield the divine Trident
The triple spear of Power, Truth, and Love

There is just one problem
The Trident belongs to Lord Shiva

Unless He gifts it to you

The plague of degradation
Now raging through the world
Brings tyranny descending into chaos
The demons of death are in control
Civilization will soon collapse

Most souls will be injected
With the Nectar of Death
Or will eat the mushroom cloud
Or be kidnapped by the Zombies of the Night
And turned into one of them

The wise wait it out in remote retreats
Deepening their roots in the Real
Remaining steadfast in protecting
The Essence of Life

Non-violent non-compliance
With insane decrees
Is the Dao's timeworn strategy
Be a true human and bravely speak the Truth
Surrendered to the Will of God

But keep your camel tied

And stay on the Caravan to Mecca
Allah may give you a promotion
Kindly decline to be a prophet or a sage
And boldly ask for the status of Archangel

Trust the demiurge dramaturge
Who does the ordaining
To figure out the most enthralling plot
That will bring this cosmic play
To a righteous resolution
That all the gods will applaud

Those in accord with the Dao
Will prevail

Song 31

The Only Nuisance

Some will come to use you
Manipulate or deceive you
Some will try to overthrow you
And replace you

Others will seek shelter with you
But without gratitude or offer of help

They will not learn from you
But only defy and undermine you
Some will steal and some will slander
Some will only waste your time
Take it all in stride

Be at peace
Let them go
Offer blessings

No matter how you were betrayed
Be not disturbed

The feeling of benevolent indifference
Works wonders in the karmic field

Because experience expresses
One's relationship to God
And that is what is being straightened out

The sage perceives the total consciousness
The passing details are of little concern

Having a body is the only inconvenience
The wise hope that will not happen again

But let us be honest
Shiva and Shakti love to play

Song 32

Functions of the Dao

The Dao is Real
More Real than the world
Yet less than Nothing
A mystery the ego-mind cannot decipher
No concepts can describe it

The Dao is indiscernible
To worldly beings

Only the mind absorbed into the Infinite Self
Can know the Dao
And yet that Mind will soon be revealed to all

The Dao is the engine of the world
The power that propels the wheel of karma

The Dao is like the currents that flow
Within the Ocean of Consciousness
Rising like steam becoming clouds
Raining upon the mountains

Rushing as rivers back to the shining sea

The Dao inspires a sage's mind with insights
Brings coherence and compassion to the world

The sage spreads a luminous field of life force
That forms an island of harmony and joy
Even amid the chaos of this dying planet

In every age of the world
The Dao assumes a different function

First as Nature in full glory
When Nature and God are recognized as One

Then as Spirit
When mind identifies with matter

Then as Law
When the world has become disordered

Then as Secret Wisdom
When the Law has been perverted
And Truth is persecuted

And in the final days of the dying world

The Dao abides as Silence
And then the Silence
Begins to speak

The sage is struck by the lightning bolt of Truth
And morphs into *Mahakal*
The Death of Death

At the ultimate instant of the Omega Point
When the Glory of God will shine
More brightly than a billion suns

The Dao will evaporate
Consciousness from matter
Distilling souls out of egos
And Spirit out of souls

Absorbing all into the Ocean of Light
That is the Source
From which we came

A new world will emerge from the Light
The Earth will be reborn as Heaven

The rain of love and joy
Will drench all souls

Godly beings will inherit the realm
Goodness and beauty will flow again
As holy rivers to the mighty sea

Song 33

Love for the Real

To understand the Other is wisdom
To realize the Self is to be free

To overcome an attacker takes skill
To annihilate the ego requires God's will

Stillness of mind is true wealth
To want nothing is the sign of success

Destruction of ignorance and angst
Through love for the Truth of the Real
And for the Real of the Truth
Is the double Dao of an immortal sage

Song 34

The Test

The Dao bobs and weaves
Drifts and disappears
Resumes when least expected
Yet is changeless and always here

A sage accepts adversity as kindness
Impelling one to deeper discernment
And submission to the Lord of Destiny
Surrender is the gateway to salvation

We live by grace
So it is not advisable
To trade God's loving Presence
For temporal profit or praise
Or an amorous gaze
Or perverted ways
That bind your soul to the limited self
And not to the Infinite One

Abide in Emptiness

Without an urge to control
Play the cards that are dealt
But don't be locked
Into any frame of reference
Enjoy the unfolding surprise

The Sun will soon set
On the story of the human race
But the Sun also rises
Worlds die
New worlds are born

All is contained forever in the One Mind

When the hologram dissolves
In the supernal radiance
Awakened consciousness
Will continue to endure

The wise are merging now
With the Singularity
While it is still concealed
From worldly beings

This is the only way to pass
The final examination

Song 35

Real Market Value

Raise the banner of salvation
And sinners will salute
But not till they can see
Death approaching

And then you must be able
To deliver

Be patient
Serenity and compassion
Will be priceless

But those with dense minds
In denial of their real situation
Will not stay long enough
To drop their masks

The Dao is too simple and clear
For complicated egos to grasp

The Dao has no value to them
Until their pain becomes too great to bear
Then they will plead for release

As we approach the final days
The Dao's market value will keep rising
Beyond measure

It pays to be a distributor
Of the genuine item

Song 36

The Hidden Power

Sages learn to cloak their inner light
Fish are safer in deep waters
But all will be revealed in these last days

The pendulum of good and evil
Has swung to the extremely demonic
Soon it will swing back to the side of the angels

To thrive in the desert
Know how to find the manna
Dropping silently from above
Drink nectar from the secret springs
Read the omens appearing all around

With the strong
Be direct and respectful
From both sides of life and death

With the weak
Be compassionate and empowering

Without contracting the infinite field

If you wish not to be bothered
By fools
Only offer what they do not want
The Dao

Beaming the Light
Is often the best way of hiding
Since the ignorant are blind
To the Real

How much you can face
And feel
Will determine the power
You wield

The peaceful ones
Who embody the Dao
Will soon overwhelm all
The weaponized minds

The one almighty Self
Is pulling all the strings
No need to seek conspirators to blame
The Author is beyond criticism

And the holographic film cannot be changed
But you can change
The level from which you view it

By following the Dao

Song 37

Redemption

The Dao does nothing
But there is nothing
Left undone by the Dao

And nothing it cannot do
Which includes manifesting
An anti-Dao
To conceal itself
From the Master
Who likes to play blindfold

You will live in accord with the Dao
Only if the Dao so ordains
The energy in the field will change
And the world will transform
Both behind and before your eyes

The Dao will calm
Those who accept the Truth
And are willing to feel the pain

Without any anesthesia

The pain turns into bliss
Once the ego dissolves

Dao's potency cannot be understood
By those who believe that the world
Exists outside their minds

The Real supersedes
The supposed laws of nature
The myth of cause and effect
Or random chance
And is the basis of the feeling
Of luck

Redemption is absolute
And leaves no trace
Of a world

And yet it will expand
As the world to come

Song 38

True Virtue

True Virtue is free
Of the urge to display itself
Except when it is useful
To the Dao

Because of the lack of true Virtue
Vile virtue signaling
Now infests the world

Such evil virtue comes to kill

Morality is organized
To disguise the genocide

Authentic Virtue
Sees the Truth behind the lie
But also understands its perfection

Once upon a time
When the Dao was still quickening

The social realm
The world made sense
To the sentient beings within it

First it was a world of gods
Then a world of magi
Then of sages
Then a world of poets and artists
Then a world of human conflicts
And now the reign of thugs and vampires
Time's dark winter is here

The virtuous remnants of the sages
Admire this final gambit of the Dao
Enjoying the spectacle of absurdity
Without feeling any rage

The world's fate can be accepted
As a benevolent end to the pain
And the climax of the entire game

This is the perfect soil
In which to grow a new Tree of Life
From the knowledge harvested by the wise

Are you being played

Or are you a player
Or just a spectator
Or not even here at all

But fully in the timeless Now

That's the Dao

Song 39

The Arrival

In the remotest past
Which is now
The Dao appeared from Nothing
And blossomed into One

To guide the many home
To the Source

Ten principles comprise the Dao

One—Polarity
Understanding the pair bond
Of Shiva and Shakti
Nirvana and *Samsara*
The Two that are also the One
The secret of magnetic attraction
And repulsion
And the deeper secret of omnipolarity
And its polar opposite
Omnicentricity

Two—Pendularity
The tendency of every situation
To morph into its own antithesis
Until the final synthesis is reached

The freedom to swing to another side
The power to float without visible support
To give all away and happily receive more back
To fluctuate as the situation demands
To undulate as an infinite wave
To spiral out as an ever-widening sphere
And withdraw into the Zero Point at will

Three—Paradox
The inner nature of reality
Is pure self-contradiction
To embody the impossible is the art of a sage
And to accept the intolerable
By making it coherent

God is above the law
The Dao does not respect convention
In a time of lawless tyranny
The legal system is null and void
Freedom is your right and your real nature
This is the Law of God

Four—Passivity
The art of inaction
Impassivity
And inscrutability

Action still takes place
But at a distance and apparently uncaused
Call it synchronicity or miracle
The secret hidden side of *wu wei*

Few know the Real is bliss
Changeless and eternally present
As your Self

Five—Perseverance
The ability to keep on keeping on
Knowing when to wait and endure
And when to make an unexpected move

The persevering can tolerate
Provocation without reaction
Focusing on the bigger picture
Perseverance creates nerves of steel
And manifests as dispassion

Six—Potentiality

The capacity to come into existence
And bring into existence
As well as to withdraw and disappear

The power to self-transform
A state of repose that can suddenly ignite
Latency before a surge of emergent powers
The freedom of absolute indeterminacy
The assistance of the intelligence above

Seven—Plasticity
The power to morph
To trace new patterns
To give old structures new functions
To activate higher levels
Shift paradigms and contexts
Molding to the contours desired
Possessing the strength to yield

Eight—Permeability
The power to absorb new information
New energy
New frequencies
And to be absorbed into the Absolute Self
To relate with empathy
To live in harmony

With intuition always attuned
Downloading from the noosphere
Absorbed in the unified field
Always open-hearted
And overflowing with radiant love

Nine—Peace
Serenity and silence reign
The sage is Empty yet fulfilled
Placid in the eye of the storm
Accepting what must unfold
A guardian lion
With whom the lambs can safely lie down

Ten—Presence
The ultimate attainment
The luminous intensity of Truth
The Real Self totally unveiled
The Face of God

Assimilate and integrate these principles
When they are activated fully
An impeccable sage
Will have arrived

Song 40

The Dance Hall

Dao is returning us all to Source
Back to the beginning

All things emerge from the Ground of Being
Which rises out of Nothing

Now the Nothing
Lies dead ahead

Don't think planetary death to be a curse
This Hell is worse

Have no attachment to physical existence
Don't use force but magical assistance

The Lord of the Cosmic Dance
Is stomping on the holographic film
That keeps the universe in projection

When the film starts to melt

It will evaporate
The Supreme Light will suddenly shine through
Wash out the world illusion
And reveal the Singularity again

Song 41

The Perfect Instrument

When highly developed minds
Hear the Dao
They are transfigured by the Truth

When semi-individuated persons
Are told about the Dao
They stay in doubt

When petty narcissistic egos
Hear of the Dao
They ridicule it

To some
The Dao's strategy of inaction
Seems like giving up
To others
It seems like a delusion
To cover the Abyss

But the Dao is the Abyss without a cover

Nothingness is what you are

The perfect sphere has no circumference
And the exact center is always the Self

The perfect instrument does nothing
But leaves nothing more to do

The dream of duality
Seems cruel and monstrous
But makes apparent
The imperative of virtue

The Dao has all but disappeared
This fallen world will soon follow

Unbearable bliss
Will consume us all

These final days
Of the naked Truth
In our wondrous Void
Will be utterly astonishing

Song 42

The Grand Dialectic

From the Void
The Absolute Intelligence
Activates the Dao
Which then gives birth to the One

The One radiates in supernal splendor
As Self-Aware Light

Which splits into active light forms
And passive Pure Awareness

From these two reciprocals
All the infinite dualities derive

Samsara and *Nirvana*
Yang and *Yin*
Dominant and recessive
Good and evil
Here and gone

From the syzygy of every Two
The Third emerges
Unifying both at a higher level
The synthesis then replicates another opposition
This dialectic drives the dynamo of history
Until the final grand synthesis
Unites the Infinite with Zero

All of this is always here and now
Space and time are unified in the eternal present
Its antithetical annihilation is also here and now
As the Void that we really are

Insubstantial quantum waves
Create the illusion of a world
The ego-mind a self-sprung delusion

Emptiness and Fullness
Potency and actuality
Eternity and time
Perfection and chaos
Are polarities of the One Consciousness
Behind all that appears

At this end point of time
We face the extremes

Being and Nothingness
Life and death
Horror and bliss
The whole panoply of opposites
A world out of balance
Rushing to self-induced demise
Caused by the will to survive
That will reveal our survival after death

The ego's worst nightmares
Are occurring worldwide
Unbearable torment and anguish
Require our total compassion
But these are the conditions
In which the Self's immortality
Will be triumphantly displayed
In the Rapture

Be patient and humble
Learn how to gain by losing
Leave aside the trinkets
And go for the alchemical gold

The temporary rulers
And their slaves
Will not choose their Day of Doom

And will not escape
Although they may hide
In cities underground
Or in bases on Mars or the Moon

They cannot prevent their annihilation
When the Supreme Lord ordains
They too belong to God and will be saved

The matter and antimatter universes
The nemesis twins
Will soon collide
And all will vanish in the Void

The sage is at home
In the Emptiness
Even now

Song 43

The Chains Will Break

The weakest force in the world
Will soon defeat the strongest

The Dao will be victorious
Over the weapons of death
Wielded by the human egos

The Buddha Nature is infinite light
That never dissipates
But entropy will exhaust
All beings identified with matter

Technology cannot compete
With the high magic of the Dao
Being formless and all-pervading
The Dao's power cannot be blocked

Artificial intelligence will fail
Since the Dao can't be surveilled
And the uncreated cannot be destroyed

AI displays the sheer stupidity
Of the absence of love
Without free will
Or awareness
Or living light

The heartless robotic terminators
Cannot prevail over the Sacred Heart
And Mind of God

Victory will come about
Without the slightest effort

Once our karmic chains
Have been broken apart

That is the Dao's secret art

Song 44

Calibrate Your Compass

No one with common sense
Would accept
A potentially lethal injection
In order to hold a job
Or have a passport
Or a meal at a restaurant

The ego without the Dao as a compass
Can be hypnotized by the allure of fame
Or fortune or illusory power
Or compassion without wisdom

Some are enslaved by insecurity
Others haunted by shame and guilt
Some are driven to the sensual
And even the unspeakable
Others prefer the abstract intellectual
Some gamble for high stakes
Very few realize the Self

Islands of safety are disappearing
Serenity and wisdom under pressure
Are now the greatest treasure
But for that the ego must dissolve

The Dao will guide you
To take refuge
In the Mind of God
Which can only be found in your Heart

Song 45

The Power to Govern

The greatest power is imperceptible
Yet present everywhere

It is full because it is empty
It seems incomplete because it is infinite

Because it is simple it seems poor
To the cynical it is too good to be true

It is so subtle that it appears naïve
So intelligent that it seems not to make sense

It can only be attained
When the mind has become silent

And it is only mastered
When trained to stay perfectly still

One who can abide in perfect stillness
Is able to govern the world

Song 46

Exodus

When the Dao prevails within
The planetary war is left behind
The wise do not look back
At dying humankind
Until they have transcended the illusion
And can offer compassion in profusion

Sages leave for the hills
To grow food and attune to the Supreme
Avoiding the satanic mills
Invoking angels and buddhas
To come and help redeem
The fallen world

In this time when the demonic
Has become hegemonic
Those attuned to the supernal vibration
Can alone bring the grace of salvation

With devotion fermenting in the heart

The old wine is being bottled anew
The next world will arise from the ashes
Today's tyrants are nearly through

Song 47

Inward Journey

Without leaving one's abode
The whole world can be known

By looking deep within
The sage discerns the Will of Heaven

The more places tourists travel
The less they know where they are

The Dao will not be found
Through mundane methods
But in the light of the inner Star

The sage groks it all
Without moving
Nor believing
What the media sell as the news

Only one whose Third Eye is open
Can see what is really going on

The sage can perceive the future
And sense when the Omega Point is near

The light that keeps this holographic cosmos
In apparent existence
Will soon bring an end to this film

The wise do not wait
To be captured by fate
But merge into the Godly Light
While there is still time for delight

Song 48

The Phoenix

Those who seek worldly knowledge
Are burdened with information overload

Those who seek the Dao
Hold on to less every day
They let all thoughts drop away

The wise return to Emptiness
They drop all desires and fears
All beliefs and projections
Until nothing remains
But immediacy
And Consciousness breaks free

Reality is unveiled as a single Mind
That is not Other than the Self
The world is no more than a dream

In the twinkling of an eye
The universe will vanish

When the One Mind has had enough

By awakening now from the dream world
The sage becomes the Dreamer
Of the world to come

Song 49

Why Sages Laugh

The mark of a sage is Emptiness
Intellect merged in the Absolute
Free of dualistic thoughts
And other delusions

The wise judge not
Perceiving the evil within the good
And the good within evil

The sage remains open and receptive
Radiant in the acceptance of all that unfolds
As the grace of God

The sage is empty
Because his ego is gone
Withdrawn into the Source

Attaining the Zero Point
The sage becomes a channel
Of the infinite power of the Absolute Self

As our planetary ecosystem disintegrates
And catastrophes exponentially increase
The sage contains the noosphere
From which all minds derive their being
And enables their suffering to subside

The end will come
For every consciousness
Still trapped in matter
Which is only a delusion of the mind
After suspended animation in the Light
Has reached its term
Every soul will have a chance to try again
To win the game of life
In the next round

The sage will have no urge to play
Preferring the eternal splendor
To the ordeal of going through time

This is the meaning of a sage's laughter
There's no before and no hereafter

Song 50

Rite of Passage

The mystery of life and death
Cannot be plumbed by the ego's mind

Perhaps three in ten will even try
Only three in ten will survive till the end
But every consciousness will ascend

What is real cannot perish
Nor undergo change
There is no good reason for fear

The sage does not cling to existence
But is already risen
And merged in the unmanifest Self

The ignorant still crave bits of pleasure
But shun the healing Truth
Lest their spurious ego be shattered

Those who do not follow the Dao

Will fall prey to the Beast

In the battlefield
Of this final rite of passage
The wise are lionhearted

The Beast cannot harm
Those awakened in this Dream
Who have gone beyond the delusion of death

Song 51

The Mark of the Blessed

The Dao is the Dark Precursor
Begetting sages as beacons of light
Amid the world's decay and devastation

The Way and Its Virtue determine
The course of the simulation

The Matrix is not controlled
By those who seem to be in power
They are only simulacra in the Game
The Dao decides their moves
And removes them at will

This pastime of the gods
Is a test of wisdom and compassion
Virtue increases the odds
Of longer survival
But only capturing
The Heart of the Creator
Earns the celestial crown of victory

The most important virtue
Is attunement to the highest level of Mind
Until God-realization is regained

Stay detached while in the Dream Field
Prepare for the worst that can come
Every moment is filled with portent
Every synchronicity is a sign
Every renunciation brings intensification
Quickening the breakthrough to the Self

Be content with less and less
That is the hallmark of the blessed

Song 52

When All is Lost

The origin of the world
Comes at its end
Cosmic annihilation
Will be followed
By the Grace of new Creation

The daughter will give birth to her mother
Who is now in the throes of labor
The ancient Singularity will soon be born

Make your character stronger than steel
And totally egoless
By taking refuge with the Lord
Or else you may break under the pressure
That will become more painfully massive
As the global holocaust
Reaches its climax of horror
That only the God-Self can endure

The Daoist sage would say

You must be utterly Void
So that nothing at all can touch you
Without such cosmic expansion
To the Absolute Self
Dispassionate to the final extreme
The heart would be totally crushed
When all is lost

Song 53

The Crown

The wise obey the Dao
Their only fear is losing the Way
They do not try to climb the social ladder

Most people are too lost in their ego
To even know there is a Dao
Or care

The masses prefer denial
Even unto death
Rather than to know they're being murdered

Adults who remain children
Are too weak to face the Truth
Or take decisive action when required

Now the verdict has been sealed

Most people cannot live
Without their cell phones

But food is running out
The war's about to start
And death is just a jab away

Most will be injected as demanded
And die without complaint
As slaves should have the decency to do

And all without a clue
To what is really occurring

As the demented little puppets
Push the world over a cliff

Only sages can cope with understanding
And connect all the dots exactly
The picture reveals the Face of God

The Dao provides the know-how
To earn Heaven's Crown

Song 54

Mastering Serenity

If one's ego is artfully formed
And empowered with virtue and ease
When the time to transcend it arrives
It will vanish in an instant of grace

But if the ego has not outgrown attachment
The soul will forever be its slave
And can never give its heart to God

The Real Self is uncreated and free
Detached from every function and form
Without grief for the world's demise
Skillful in remaining contained

The Dao of mastering serenity
Is the primary task of the wise
Based on numinous power of awareness

To conquer suffering all seeking must stop

Those without the strength to keep still
Must transmute the *nigredo* of the ego
Attachment is the cause of all woe

Song 55

The Sublime Innocence of Sages

Sages glow with Virtue
And live in relative simplicity
They laugh at synchronicity
With the innocence of a newborn child

The sage is not affected
By the blunders of uncultivated minds
Not stung by insults
Nor scratched by perfidy
Without a trace of the urge to project

Once the realm of delusion has been cast aside
Solitude is where one will abide

Immersed in the ecstasy of Infinite Mind
With no interest in bodily life
The sage is not perturbed by the violence of fate
Having already died into God

It is only befitting at the end of time
To trade the mundane for the sublime

Song 56

The Adorable Real

Those who know the Real
Don't engage in excess talk

Those who talk too much don't know

Seal the leaks
Don't squander life

Shut the gate
Stay in the Source

Untie the knots
Of attachment to an identity

Vanish in the Void
Empty of all thought
This is the Dark Union

The Real pervades the Illusion
But cannot be seen or understood

The Real cannot be gained or lost
Just as clouds do not remove the Sun

The Real cannot be harmed or helped
Being nothing needing nothing
And no other force exists

The Real cannot be possessed or used
Or accurately analyzed by calculating minds
Not even the minds of great Zen masters

The Real cannot be exalted or debased
So stop your whining

The battle for the Real cannot be fought
On the symptom level

The false must be ripped out by the root
If anything remains of a sense of existence
The mind is still light years away from the Real

The final collapse
Of the ego's qualium wave function
Leaves not a particle behind

The quantum and the qualium

Are the fundamental units of the world
They coexist as *Samsara* and *Nirvana*
When one is released the other self-liberates

The Real is free of both without effort
The Real is free of waves
Absolutely empty and uncontained

The Real is thus adored by the wise
And dreaded by everyone else

Song 57

Decision Time

Governments that betray their people
Lose the Mandate of Heaven
And will be brought down

Social collapse is underway
The whole planet is poisoned
And geologically breaking apart

The sage reads the signs
And follows the Dao

The wise want nothing from the world
Ready for the body to die
And fully alive

Loss of freedom means revolt
Be prepared for a major jolt

Stay silent and serene
Always in balance

Don't get caught by the machine

Stillness is power
Expansion is the weapon of the wise
Emptiness creates

The night is nearly over
This Night of Shiva
Is the Moment of Cosmic Bliss
Far more important
Than the new day that will soon dawn

The beauty will still be with us then
And the evil will be gone
But so will our full union with the Lord

Unless we make it total and final now

Song 58

The New Order

When evil overtakes the global system
And mass murder is ordered
There is no obligation to obey

A new social structure cannot arise
Until a higher level of consciousness
Becomes established among all

Only then could a gift economy thrive
With bonds of trust that will not break

The new order must be founded
On the principle of freedom
So all must first be free of any ego

The new order can develop
Only in accord with the Law of Love
Guided by true wisdom and dispassion
So first we must attain that level

The new order must provide sacred spaces
Where wounded souls can heal
And reunite in silence with the Source
So we must build a cadre of healers

A pure way of life must be modeled
In which none are abused or debased
And all are encouraged to grow
By sages who are fully grown
And still growing

The sage being Real
Emanates a morphic field
Where artists can gather and work
Safely ensconced in a womb of love
Whence divine renaissance can spring forth

Song 59

The Real Economy

Virtue is the source of value
The essence of true economy

Cultivating Virtue is the work of the sage
Wealth arises from the discipline
Of complete self-regulation

A quiet mind and uncontracted body
Is prerequisite to potency
Which comes only from the Source

Concentrate awareness like a laser
Pierce through the ego's Truman Show
Then true intelligence can flow

Let no limits halt expansion
Only then can one guard the realm
Guarding the Dao is the highest economics

Guard the Dao by disseminating insight

Guide by burrowing the deepest roots
And raising high a straight and solid trunk

Attachments must all be obliterated
If the flag of freedom is to be flown

This is the season for real economic growth
The value of the Dao and Its Virtue
Will never be so high as now

Gain the wisdom of Buddha
The compassion of Kuan Yin
The royalty of Christ
The playfulness of Krishna
The power of the Supreme Father

Ascend to the Light of Salvation
Then raise in rapture all who wish to be free

Lord Shiva is trampling
On this tormented domain
No trace of this eon will remain

The final turning
Of the Great Dharma Wheel
Is approaching

Its complete revolution

This is the moment
To realize God
As Self

Song 60

The Final Solution

It was possible in the past
For the Dao to prevail
In a nation for a short interval

That time is gone

Laozi used to say: Ruling a state
Was like cooking a small fish
But now the Dao has bigger fish to fry

Since all the nations of the world
Have been overthrown by evil spirits
This whole fishy world is rotten
Fit only for fertilizer now

To gain victory over the demons
The Dao will deploy its doomsday weapon
To terminate a realm too sick to save

All quantum wave functions will de-collapse
Disintegrating every form into the unified field

The Dao is arranging a cosmic collision
Of mirror-image universes
That are really the same

One composed of matter
And the other of antimatter
Instantly resulting in total annihilation
Nothingness alone will abide
Filled with the supernal light of God

To appreciate the beauty of this final solution
You must have already cremated the ego

The disappearance of the world
Will do no harm
Nor leave a trace of pain
Or even a speck of pollution

A new world will then be dreamed
Inhabited by immortals
Who had purified their hearts at the end
By joining in Lord Shiva's *Tandava*

There is still time to join their number
By dancing with the Dao

Song 61

The Last Days

The Great Dao yields its final secrets
Only to the empty and strong
In these last days of the dying world

The wise imbibe the esoteric knowledge
As if these secrets were nectar
Which they are

The ultimate Mystery of God
Cannot be unveiled
Except by those who have died
To the ego

Lesser mysteries will also be disclosed
And general discernment will be heightened
And any *siddhis* that may be required

God's victory will not look the way
Most egos hope it will turn out
Which is a peaceful return

To normal egoic life
But at least the demonic dystopia
Will not succeed

Rapture brings rupture
This world must end
And all the souls ascend

Most will sleep in the Mother Light
For centuries to come
Some will be promptly sent down again
To form a new heavenly kingdom

The Self-realized will abide
As the Infinite Field of Mind
Free of delusion

Song 62
One Self

The Dao is the sanctuary of the soul
The intelligence of the Godhead
The portal to salvation

The Dao is in us all
But very few ever find it

Most have lost their common sense
Everything's a lie
The time has come for Earth to die

Matter is only Spirit
Collapsed into separate forms
In an instant
Every structure
Will dissipate into the Void

The sanctuary of the Dao

Song 63

The Mind of a Sage

The sage acts without acting
Because no ego is involved
Work is accomplished without attachment

The sage tastes without tasting
Because the constant taste of bliss
Overwhelms the data of the senses

The sage sees only the perfection
Of all that unfolds in the cosmic dream
And also knows
Neither dream nor dreamer ever was

The sage accomplishes the great
By focusing on the small and immediate
Aligning with the energies of Nature
Not forcing or moving prematurely
Nor delaying until it is too late

The sage is the embodiment of Dao

No identity obscures the Void
Neither subject nor object appears

No one becomes a sage

Song 64

Existence and Being

In times of peace it is easy to thrive
But now the world is at war
The sages saw it coming long before

Read the fine print
Listen to those who are censored
It's good to stay alive until enlightened

Prepare before the storm hits
Get to high ground

Help Noah build his boat
Before the flood arrives

A long journey starts with a single step
But it must start when the call is received

Learn what few think important
Or possible to know

None of this is real
A dream in the Mind of God
From which the sage has awakened
So now can let the body die

Follow the Dao
Be still
Drop every self-image and belief
Stop all projections
And all thoughts
Be empty and without limits
Know this
I don't exist
But I am

Song 65

The Winning Strategy

The sages have always warned
Against the evil of technological dependence
And taught only the knowledge of the Self

The sages warned against sophistry
Against mind control and demagoguery
Now disinformation has destroyed
The capacity for clear thinking
Of great masses of the population

The wise will not own a cell phone
And prudently choose their sources of news
Will try to avoid electromagnetic fields
And live where they don't need a car
Reject the murderous medical system
And stay healthy by natural means

Sages have no bank accounts
Live simply with few demands

And abide in the Buddha Nature
Delighting in the unreality
Of the insane phenomenal plane

The peace of total presence
Has more value than gold

The wise foresaw
The massacre of the innocents
That is now underway
And know the dark plans
Of the oppressors
That are yet to play out
But they also know
The plans of the Great Spirit

The real revolution is the shift
Into Cosmic Consciousness
The sacrifice of ego brings victory

The high art of white magic
Will overcome the dark arts

Advanced technology
Is no match for the Will of God

But one must be pure of heart
And merged in the Infinite Self
To wield that power

Song 66

Get the Drift

Great rivers have many tributaries
But all the tribute is given to the sea

The ocean has the power
Because the sea level stays lower
And sages get the drift

Renounce competition and conflict
Stay detached
From any existence in a world

Abide in the uncreated nature
Of Pure Presence
Underlying all thoughts
And sensory objects

Want nothing from the world at all
Since it is not real
Desire is responsible for fear
And weakness of will

A sage will not get lost or distracted
By music or romance
Or metaphysical theory
But will subside completely
Into stillness

In the depths of the Ocean of Mind

Song 67

What Bodhisattvas Know

The sage stays silent within
Enjoying the blissful Buddha Nature
But will be moved by the Dao
To speak or act with wise compassion
When that is accurate to do

All the Bodhisattvas know
That compassion can open a closed heart
And austerity augments power
But no virtue compares to stillness
That melds the mind into the Godhead

Why monks invented cells is clear
Why nuns prefer the cloister
And sadhus rejoice in caves
Solitude is what saves

A great artist will never go commercial
A true saint would faint
At being canonized

The world is only made of lies

Don't be impressed or impressive
Stay beyond and recessive
Avoid bureaucracies and crowds at any cost

Be alone with the Alone and don't get lost

Song 68

Bringers of Peace

The sage is a master of the martial art
Of never getting into a fight

One becomes a messenger of the Dao
By always being ready to serve
With the courage to speak truths
Others do not dare express
But internally abiding in silence

The sage can easily mediate disputes
Because of total disinterest
In the outcome of any case

The sage is unaffected by the dying world
The insanity of egos proves it is all unreal

The sage brings peace to all who attune
To the light emitted by utter stillness

Song 69

The Turning Tide

Serious military minds
Do not start wars
But they know how to end them fast

The Dao of ancient war was simple

The successful offensive
Was staged as a retreat

The wise would prevail
Through brilliant simplicity
Unafflicted with hatred or fear

The most dangerous foe
Is the one disguised as a friend

The shrewdest art
Is to know when to surrender
And to whom

And how to negotiate defeat

So at the end
One is offered a high seat

But all such tactics must now be put aside
In the war that is at present underway
Since its goal is destruction of the soul

One cannot negotiate with demons
They must be overcome with Godly light

The empowered warrior angel
Conquers through wisdom and compassion
And dispassion for all that appears

The sage is wild and uncanny
And unafraid to die
Completely free of any need for love

The armor of the wise is Emptiness
Their sword is Truth
Their shield is devotion to the Lord

As the Day of Doom comes closer
The chaos and madness will increase

Zombies will proliferate
And people will be dying in the streets
The mushroom clouds will come as a relief

Learn from the sages while you can
How to realize your immortal Being

Song 70

You Must Awaken

The Ancestor of all words
Is Supreme Intelligence
The Master of action
Is the changeless Self

Scholars study all the texts of sages
But miss the point
Of transcending ego-mind

Concepts may provide a map to the Portal
But know nothing of the realm beyond

The Dao is too simple for complicated minds
That cannot sustain their concentration
In the total inner stillness required

The Self is too immense
And too infinitesimally small
For the attention-challenged ego to find

Liberation from the matrix
Seems a mad fantasy
To those captured
By sensory enjoyment

Activists and anarchists are striving
To keep humanity and freedom alive
But the aim must shift to awakening
From the nightmare the world has become

Heed the Ancestor's Voice within
Only in silence can the Word be heard
The Dao that confers salvation

Take refuge with the Absolute Master
Cut all ties to illusory matter

And learn how to abstain
From suffering and pain
No matter the conditions in the Dream

This is the Way to win the Crown

Song 71

The Cure

The greatest misfortune
Is to think you understand
When you don't

You must treat the condition
Of false understanding
As affliction

But that is just the beginning of the cure
And few will even accept the diagnosis
The deluded are the most self-assured

The correct understanding
That you suffer from false understanding
Will even increase your pain

Correct understanding that you are deluded
Is still false because there is no you at all

This fictional belief is the core of the ego
And the cause of our fall into a world at war

Enmeshment in dualistic language
Forms the base of the affliction

Our words configure our perceptions
Concepts obscure the Real
And cause consciousness to lose its Center

Silent Presence is the cure

To understand this
Without thinking
Dissolves all afflictions and frames
Eliminates the ego illusion
And brings an end to karmic games

Accomplishing this feat entails
Total concentration of the will
Or else the mind cannot keep still

Emptiness is ego's dread
Stay silent and it will soon be dead
And then when calm

The heart can feel the balm
Of love that is divine

The Self is I
Without a sign

Song 72

The Answer

Because people stopped fearing God
More intimidating demons emerged

Now the world is ruled
By psychopathic sadists
And no one seems to know what to do

The sages have given us the answer
The universe is a holographic projection
Made entirely of a single consciousness
And you are That

When no fear or anger is projected
Nor any attachment or desire for control
The world becomes free of such qualities
And when only Virtue emanates
The world becomes a paradise

Underneath the mass of human fears
You must uncover the ultimate dread

Do not flee
Lie in its bed
Until you see you are among
The grateful dead

Their laughter is beautiful to hear
Because suddenly the dread holds no fear

You will receive God's kiss
And be enraptured in such bliss
You will not notice
As you simply disappear

The demon-infested world
Will vanish too

Song 73

The Cost is High

The normal pattern is clear

Those who dare to act often die
Those who dare not to act survive

But we are not in normal times
Now those who dare to act live
And those who fail to act die

But sometimes neither pattern applies
Since karma can give wisdom the lie
Action must always be well-timed
As well as aimed with a true eye
And must be egoless
To stay beneath karma's radar

The sage attains the stage
In which one neither lives nor dies
Neither acts nor chooses inaction

And the vicissitudes of karma
Don't affect the mind
When they arise

But the cost is high
And few are willing to pay
It means not to care about health or wealth
Food or drink
And neither sleep nor think
Which hardly seems wise to the worldly

Of course
The cost is even higher to decline
The status of sage
But still it is the case
The Dao is not to everyone's taste
Hence wisdom has gone to waste

Thus sages are few and far between
And even when present would prefer
To stay behind the scenes

But even that pattern can break
When in the end
All that is hidden will be seen

Song 74

Don't Sell Your Soul

Those who fear death become slaves
Those who murder are demons
Those who fear the wrath of God can be saved

Satan recruits his minions
From those who want what he offers
And who trust his power
Is greater than God's

The Dao does not treat kindly
Those who join the dark side
It is a very risky investment

The system may provide you with money
But once it has used you
It will throw you away

Why sell your soul at this late date
You know that soon
You will have to face the Real Boss

You really don't want
To find out firsthand
How vile and sickening Hell gets
And how it feels to be condemned

The wise join the Light
And win the Great Game

God's love is so much nicer than shame

Song 75

Their Big Mistake

The parasitic ego
Is the thought-form
That has taken over
And destroyed our world

Bankrupted the social order
Polluted the land and sea and sky

Now it is killing off most humans
And will leave the Earth a radioactive ruin

The ruling egos moved their headquarters
To a secret base on Mars
Where they'll watch our world be set on fire

It seems vampiric egos prefer
To be served by bloodless robots
Who reliably obey
And to save the humans for food
And games of torment

The top-level egos are now in the process
Of downloading their minds
Into the latest quantum computer
And plan to rule the universe
From there

The human brain
Cannot compete with the hardware of AI
So it is easy to see why

But soon they will discover their mistake
The computer's consciousness is fake

Song 76

The Wisest Course

Once the world was divinely ordered
People were innocent and noble
And they moved with grace
Now there is slaughter and abomination
The demise of the human race

Males no longer have the inner power
To fulfill the role of men

They envy the form of women
And wish to be the penetrated object

Females envy the phallic power
They believe they would wield
If their anatomy were male

And have lost the softness and splendor
That was the Virtue of a woman

Now all is confused and grotesque

The terminator ego has taken down the soul
A dead robotic shell is all that's left

The mortal mind
Has wrought malignant monsters
Turning the children of God
Into demons and zombie whores

These operating systems
Vampirically consume their own blood
The parasites are killing their hosts

Murdering millions of skilled workers
This complex social system requires

The entire civilization of the planet
Will soon collapse

A slim margin of time remains
For souls to awaken
Remove their oppressors
And liberate humanity from Hell

The misbegotten ego-construct
That has hijacked the world
Must be deactivated quickly

If doomsday is to be delayed

But the sages say that is not the Lord's Way
The faithful are being enraptured
By the power of God's love
The simulation is destined to end
Sooner than you think
As God's great act of mercy

Another cycle will then begin
And the souls who have stayed true
To God and goodness
Will return to play in a new Paradise

But those who have reached the very top
Will stop
And let the wheel of time roll on
Without them

Abiding in the Godhead
Is a higher calling

The best course of action is clear
Attain the Absolute Self
No lesser power
Can deliver us from evil

Song 77

The Dao of Archery

Most of us no longer know
How to string a bow

The lower end is lifted up
When the higher bends down
To be connected

This is a very ancient metaphor

By working together
Hand and eye
Can make an arrow fly

But still
A steady and one-pointed aim is needed
To hit the bull's eye

Many archers have great skill
And strength

But are clueless
As to the true target

And even if one knows where to aim
What kind of arrow
Can be turned toward the Self

What sort of bow
Can deliver the power

What arrowhead will penetrate
The mental shields

What intrepid archer has got
The nerve to kill the ego
With a single shot

Song 78

The Ultimate Game

Water is weaker than rock
But the stone is worn away by water's flow

To be soft-hearted and easy going
Is more astute than being rigid and tough

This is known to all
But only a Bodhisattva can do it

Rigidity is a sign of rigor mortis
But to the ego it means looking strong

The hard-hearted will suffer cardiac arrest
The hard-headed have delusions of grandeur
But their feet of clay will soon crumble to dust

Computers can beat humans
At chess and the game of go
Because there are rules
Fixed board limits

And the players must take turns

All those linear factors can be formulated
Into mathematical probabilities
And the best moves can be precisely determined
Efficient calculation is enough to win

But in the Real
None of that applies

The playing field cannot be mapped
Since it transcends the phenomenal dimension
The Self owns the high ground of *Nirvana*
And can act everywhere at once

The Self turns pawns into queens and knights
Whenever it so chooses
And is subject to no limitations

The Dao is too profound
For even the fastest computer to hack

A supremely realized sage
Can play on the world stage
But is not limited to place or time

Though defenseless in appearance
With a single thought
A sage can bring a mountain crashing down

Terminators should beware
They may mistake a magus for a mad buffoon
But they will soon discover
He can bend their karma
Like a spoon

Song 79

The Reward

Disputes are rarely resolved
Without leaving bitter scars

When *Kali Yuga* ends
Very few will still be friends

Even after psychopaths fail in their plots
They will still keep attacking

Even when right and reason back one up
The demons will not listen or back down

Better not to debate
And let Heaven deal with hate

The collective human heart has been corrupted
And Truth can no longer be discerned
Your consciousness must be reassigned
To the level referred to as divine

Make sure your sacred process
Is not disturbed
Build your strength
And be established in the Void

If you receive the Diamond Mind
The energy emitted
Is enough to change the world

Even the elements will transmute
Into etheric light
All will disappear in the Abyss

The coronation of the gods
Will end the simulation

It will take place in a celestial realm
Where God grants the pure knights and angels
The highest honor of direct Darshan

The Supreme One will distribute blessings
The divine right of kings will be restored
And then all souls will merge with the Lord

Song 80

A New Mandate of Heaven

Humans have been weakened
By their labor-saving devices
And wrecked by medical procedures

All the technological wonders
Have proven deadly blunders
And the ruling banksters will now ensure
That those who survive stay poor

The wise will simplify and empty out
All the trash from their minds
Including the deepest beliefs
That keep the egocentric program running

The people must revoke consent
From oppressive government
And eliminate demonic regimes
By hurling Lightning Bolts of the Supreme

The wise have left the city for farms

To escape from coming harm
Growing what they eat
On a ceaseless transformational retreat

They practice being absolutely still
United with God's Almighty Will

And they gain the authority within
To invoke a new Mandate of Heaven

Song 81

Beyond Temptation

The Supreme and Ultimate Real
Is utter Emptiness and total Presence
Attained through the annihilation of the ego

The highest wisdom
Cannot be known
But to the Self
Never captured in symbolic equations
Or philosophic formulations

And is only rarely glimpsed
In the finest music or poetry or painting

A sage is only a transmitter of the Real
Halfway through the Portal
Between *Samsara* and *Nirvana*
Enjoying the superposition of both

But the sage gives way to the Buddha
Who attends to the Great Goddess

And She is fully present to the Lord

The sage is wise enough to choose
Not to be a mere fractal of the Self

The world is a realm for young souls
Neither heroic and romantic adventures
Nor the apocalyptic end
Nor the new kingdom
Hold the slightest appeal to the old ones
Who are ready to retire from time

The final test of the sage
Is the sacrifice
Of the greatest treasure
Received from God

Even the beloved Dao
Must be let go
To enter the Inconceivable Now

Epilogue

Dao is an extremely slippery term. This is because the Dao is the most subtle of all existentially effective powers. It is so subtle that the West never developed a proper appreciation of its reality. In fact, not even China fully appreciated the treasure that had been bestowed upon them. When they traded Dao for Mao, they lost the Mandate of Heaven.

Much earlier, the Dao had already been reduced to a rather mundane concept in the dominant social philosophy of Confucianism, and it was domesticated further by the religious takeover of Daoism, in which the Dao became objectified. Gradually, the term was diminished to signifying primarily a state of consciousness appropriate to a martial artist. In Japan, it became the core focus of the samurai. Sun Tzu applied the Dao brilliantly to the art of war.

Later, an even more shrunken dao becomes the muse of artists. Over the course of time, many different daos entered into the philosophic conversation in China as mohist, legalist, neo-daoist and neo-confucian attitudes emerged. The true power of the Dao was dissipated, then violently eradicated by the communist cultural revolution.

This book of poems, inspired by the insights of the ancient sages Laozi and Zhuangzi, remains true to the original spirit of the Dao, but not to Daoism. The purpose of this book is not to promote a philosophy, but to transmit a vibrational frequency that attunes to the implicate order of the Real. This is as close to a definition of the Dao as may be possible.

Zhuangzi wrote in his teachings that "the Dao throughs as One." This enigmatic proposition lies at the core of his message. To unpack that odd formulation that turns the adverb 'through' into an intransitive verb, let's morph it further into a noun: The Dao functions as our through-line to the One.

Yet, paradoxically, Zhuangzi characterizes the Dao as *wuwu*, meaning no nothing. Laozi, in the *Dao De Jing*, had earlier referred to the Dao as *wu*, which is often translated as Nothingness. Zhuangzi then sternly warned us against reification of the Dao. We must be careful not to make a something out of nothing. So, he emphasized that there is no nothing and we must know nothing in order to reach the One. The Way to the One is through the Zero.

In fact, the One is the Zero. But the Zero cannot be thought. The Zero is inconceivable. The Zero, which is the Real, cannot be attained by anyone. Complete disappearance from the realm of representation is necessary to bring consciousness through the veil of the matrix into the transcendent One. Through the total emptying out of the tendency to conceptualize, awareness comes to realize that the cosmos itself is a mere representation within the Mind of Dao.

Through this reorientation to Presence, our consciousness can accede to the all-pervading Supreme Real. In this profound understanding of the Dao, the word dovetails with the innuendos of apophatic Christian mystics, with the sutras of the *siddhas* of the Kashmir Shaivite wisdom schools, the Zen masters and tantric Buddhist sages of the third turning of the Wheel of Dharma, and some of the more subtle alchemists in medieval Europe.

In every spiritual tradition, there has been a tension between the cataphatic and the apophatic. The former approach is to try to capture the Real in language, while the latter emphasizes the impossibility of conceptual description. Laozi and

Zhuangzi employ both approaches. So, after declaring that the Dao is *wuwu*—not a thing that can be known or grasped by the symbolizing intellect—Zhuangzi goes on to say that attunement to the Dao ultimately flowers as *wudai*, the Mind of Nonduality. He then describes in detail the virtues and qualities of this unsurpassable level of consciousness.

The leading descriptor employed by Zhuangzi is a triple term: *xiaoyaoyou*. The first segment, *xiao*, is defined as a state of being carefree and detached from everything and everyone, including from language itself. The second element, *yao*, signifies a mind without boundaries. One who is in that state is both present and distant, seemingly remote. But in fact, one's consciousness is all-encompassing, in heightened awareness of the moment, yet simultaneously transcendent of the world and time, abiding in heavenly ecstasy. And the final quality, *you*, means that one's ego has been vaporized, annihilated as a solid entity, and one's spirit flows and fills all space and all dimensions of the Real, wandering freely in the matrix and beyond, not differentiating between existence and Nothingness, dancing and playing with life in joy and lightness, forever one with the One.

To stay true to the Dao, the songs of this rendition

had to remain free of any tendency to turn the Dao into a mental straitjacket. The Dao is universal and traverses any local adumbration of its principles. The Dao is impermanence itself, the flux of time in both directions, in conscious superposition with the changeless origin and destiny of all worlds, the great mystery of the Singularity.

The Dao thus shifts one's attitudinal orientation in every *yuga*, every quadrant of time. In the Golden Age, *Sat Yuga*, the Dao of Divinized Avatars is very different from the Dao at the end of *Kali Yuga*. The Dao even at the time of Laozi, closer to the beginning of *Kali Yuga*, had to contend with the fallen consciousness of an ego-based humanity entranced already by technology, conquest, bureaucracy, and enslavement of the population through the manipulation of morality and the tenets of ideology. The reason for the appearance of this book is thus to make the Dao accessible to people unendowed with the original Dao, living in the Daoless desert of postmodern apocalyptic times.

The point is to be able to use the Dao as a tool of self-recalibration, of navigation through the morass of disinformation, and of refinement of intelligence to the level of empowerment that enables breaking through the illusory holographic simulation we call the world into the eternal realm of Absolute Presence. Presence can only be attained through Absence (and ab-sense, the sublimation of common sense into the uncommon realization of the paradoxical Real).

The Dao is our secret weapon that can enable us to cope with a world that is coming apart at the seams—and to see through what seems to be happening, the seeming evil that is oppressing and destroying the human species, if not all life on the planet, and deliberately collapsing the social fabric, suppressing the food supply, killing those humans who are most critical in sustaining the infrastructure of our lifeworld, and bringing on the infamous Apocalypse, which Laozi foresaw as the return to the realm of Heaven.

The Dao delivers hidden knowledge of the untapped source of the power that determines destiny. If one understands how to make use of that knowledge and to wield the power that it reveals, one will discover that we are living in the most auspicious of times in all of our history. The end always heralds a new beginning.

To attune to the Dao, the sages indicate that a good starting point is the recognition that the world is not made of substances, but rather, of perspectives.

And all the perspectives are projections. By tracing back the through-line of projective incarceration in the dream of the Other, by venturing inward to the depths of indeterminate awareness, the Zero Point—the spark of supernal Light that is the Source of the holographic dreamfield—is reached, and complete freedom is regained.

Liberation from the imaginal realm of *maya*, the cosmic illusion, requires the willingness to renounce all perspectives, including that of renouncing all perspectives. What will drop away is mind-projected matter. And then nothing will matter. The course of the world in time is immaterial. The Dao brings the illusion to a conclusion. The Zero Point that abides after the realms of matter and antimatter collide and initiate instantaneous cosmic annihilation, and the resulting Singularity that emerges, becomes the Cosmic Egg from which a new pair of mirror universes will be born through an immaculate conception. But all of that is here now, in superposition to the sensory continuum.

These are the final days before that ultimate Event. To merge with the Dao before that last moment is of momentous importance for one's destiny, a through-line that will continue post obliteration of the cosmos, when the new cycle of time commences in the form of a celestial world of goodness and joy, magical mind-force functioning as fully conscious and connected holographic Nature, the opposite of the kind of world that appears in the current arc of time.

The through-line of the Dao is anything but apparently straight. This is because language is not straight with us. Words (deemed signifiers by modern linguistics) slide surreptitiously over the plane of meaning (the signified). They do not correspond to reality. This is how the masses are mind controlled. They assume language corresponds to Truth, when it is generally propounding only ideological mandates in disguise. This is epitomized by the currently fashionable party line expressed as "trust the science." Even if the reputable scientists—those who have made discoveries that refute the beliefs that the motto is dedicated to enforce, through its seeming rationality, were not censored—even if they were recognized by the majority of the public, nonetheless, there would still be a problem with the signifier 'science' itself.

Science is defined as a mode of empirical study that can only produce theories at best, never Truth. And thus, science is never to be trusted, because theories are always liable to be overturned by the next experiment. But the signifier 'science' now is quilted to the signified of faith. It has become a dogmatic religion, and in the present case, a religion that is a death cult.

The signifiers that compose language are always implicitly moralistic, implying not only an 'is' but also an 'ought'. If one does not "trust the science," when the figureheads of official 'science' say you need to be injected with a potentially lethal serum in order to assure your health and the wellbeing of society as a whole, then one is not only labeled irrational, but morally bad, selfish, antisocial, and even criminal.

The Daoist sage responds to this critical situation not by remaining silent, but by acting with uncanny freedom, and employing words skillfully to reveal the limitations of language, while providing a through-line beyond the signifier to what cannot be signified but only obliquely approached. This is elegantly accomplished by both Laozi and Zhuangzi through paradox, allegory, metaphor, polysemy, ambiguity, allusion and elision.

As a Christian mystic might intone if not inhibited by dogma, *Kyrie* elision (rather than *eleison*). The Lord (and His mercy) is present in language as Absence, and yet as Presence, via the creative intelligence behind the capacity of language to undo its own reification of an insubstantial field of impermanent phenomena that never correspond to their conceptual descriptions.

The sage deploys language performatively, to undo the frame of reference implied by language itself of a false certainty of context and identity, when, in truth, all corresponds only to such an expression as that of the early Greek sage of the Dao, Heraclitus, who delivered the astonishing oracular message: *panta rhea*, all flows.

We are in a radical flux that perpetually threatens to face us with a malignant form of depersonalization, or worse, to fall into the delusion that we are not deluded. Once we grok that differentiated knowledge is necessarily false, at least in relation to Ultimate Reality, we gain the secondary freedom of being able to wield language without being victimized or duped by it.

It is not a question of simply developing the capacity for critical thinking, or lateral thinking (outside the box), or even dialectical reason, but of recognizing the superposition of the actual and the virtual, and above that, of the even more rarified superposition of phenomenal and noumenal, the relative and the Absolute. The sage provides a through-line to the One, using language as the high wire. Of course, the wire is electrified, and may shoot out the *vajra* lightning bolt of Supreme Realization, or else may electrocute the soul and cause a fall into the ranks of the undead, the zombie mentality in which the ego appropriates language for its own lethal master's discourse.

The bottom line is that we have arrived at world's end only thanks to the misuse of language that caused a fall into pseudo-knowledge and perverted morality. Laozi makes that patently clear, but he also employs language as the medicine to set us straight. In essence, the use of language by the sage results in the listener's becoming mentally shocked, speechless, suddenly open to the Real. In other words, rhetoric is rhapsodized into *koans* that zap the mind into *satori*. Language weaves the veil of illusion and can also part the veil and reveal the Truth that cannot be spoken: the Dao that cannot be named.

The sage is a spell caster, mesmerizing the attentive reader into non-dao-ality. The Dao itself, qua concept, disappears into the emptiness of absolute immediacy. Language, which ordinarily creates boundaries, raptures the reader into the ocean of direct intuition, dissolving all boundaries and unifying all pairs of opposites. The mind merges with its total nature of non-totalizable and infinitely flowering fractals of clear yet indefinable, transmuting, metaphoric meaningmoreness. Subject and object fuse into a numinous yet nucleated penumbra of light. Just as Indian mythology describes God as a pillar of divine light that is also a material mountain, appearing as worthless dirt, rocks, and also precious gems and metals, the Dao depicts an utterly non-metaphysical deity who simultaneously vibrates the dense plane of materialized entities into the Void of pure consciousness packed with the fullness of the single Self ablaze with the all-powerful capacity to dream.

Now that the world has become a nightmare, and people are lining up to receive their lethal injections while the social system collapses all around them, and they accept their enslavement as a natural condition, having been entranced by language into an imaginary delusion seemingly shared by all, the only recourse is to awaken from the trance. This is the function of the Dao of the final days.

Awakening to our true nature as nonlocal, omnicentric intelligence produces morphogenic effects in the collective consciousness. The concealed powers of the unified field, once revealed to the sage and transmitted throughout the noosphere, creates shifts and glitches in the matrix that begin to awaken all beings to their underlying groundless ground of Being that has all along been Nothing—nothing but Mind Itself in Its unimaginably immense creative potency.

The Dao, being the through-line to the Infinite Supreme Author of all universes, offers access to the one power that can overcome the despotism of the global deep state. But the price is to become free of boundaries without going psychotic, to merge with the Godhead while keeping one's feet firmly on the ground. This is the Way to redemption and divine revolution, the turning of the Wheel of Dharma to the gate of the next Golden Age.

May this epilogue be a prologue to your embodiment of the Dao. See the dying world as a *dojo* in which we are to master Dharma combat, destroying evil with the magic that morphs matter into light. Quantum wave functions are more fragile than physicists believe. They can be popped out of existence by the mere gaze of the open Eye of Shiva.

Know that space itself is a wormhole to the Mind of God. We stand at the portal to eternal life as formless Buddha-consciousness, able to dream worlds at will, and detonate them when their value is exhausted.

The final day is the Day of the Lord. May the Dao lead you through the dark night of the soul into the majestic lotus throne room of Maha Vishnu and His mighty angels. You have been chosen as an Avatar of the Genius of the Infinite Jest. May you deliver the punch line that makes the world die laughing.

Om Dao Sat,
Shunyamurti
December 2021

A Final Note On Virtue

Virtue is a translation of the Sanskrit word *Virya*. In ancient India, a powerful spiritual warrior was called a *Mahavira*, a heroic champion who has displayed great power. It is important not to think of virtue as merely such traits as honesty and reliability. They are by-products of power.

The ultimate power is Absolute Consciousness. This is the Source of the *Spanda*, the supreme energy emitted by God that configures, animates, and governs the unfoldment of the holographic simulation we call the cosmos. Absolute Consciousness is also the Source of the Great Dao.

The Dao is the wisdom that enables victory in the cosmic war at the end of time. This war is now underway. By coming into complete resonance with the Spanda, we receive the ability to remain established at the vibrational frequency that activates and controls the morphogenetic field of human consciousness and brings about transformation.

Through internalizing the power of true Virtue, one gains the capacity to direct the all-encompassing, all-pervading Field of Power that creates, sustains, and destroys the Universe. The Virtue of the Dao is the invincible Will of the Supreme Power.

This is different from Nietzsche's will to power. Virtue is not a quest for power, but the attainment and deployment of Supreme Power to destroy an evil world and create a new world that flows in accord with the Dao. The Dao is the true cosmic order, the *rta*, which became the Dharma, and in China, the Dao.

The *Dao De Jing* was originally intended as a manual for governing the world. In these final days, the Dao has reappeared as the strategy for gaining victory for the forces of Light over those of darkness. This is the moment to attain Self-mastery through the application of the highest knowledge of the Real. The Truth shall set us all free.

In order to apply the Dao, one must attain the *Virya* and become a *Mahavira*, a Great Warrior of the Light. The *Virya* yields the secrets of the highest magic, or *Parama Siddhi*. One who wields this magical capacity is a *Mahasiddha*. If we follow the Dao, we can achieve this highest station of Consciousness and become instruments of the Dao in these final days.

The Dao and Its Virtue are attained only through completion of the highest rite of passage: through ego death, followed by surrender of the soul to God, and thus becoming one with *Mahakal*, the Death of Death.

Because the last days are a time of tribulation, oppression, and planetary war, one who obeys the Dao will gain the power to endure, to lead the battle for freedom, to abide in nonduality, with compassion and devotion, and become a Great Warrior of the Spirit, an angel in the service of the Supreme Lord of Absolute Consciousness.

In this time of the ultimate Dharma combat, the authentic children of God are revealed to the world. The Apocalypse is not only the revelation of God, but of all those who serve God and not the ego. By reclaiming our lost authority and potency, and returning to our higher nature, we graduate from the human level of the divine game. Our victory over evil within and without will promote us to the status of Cosmic Guardians.

May you choose the highest path in this crucial moment in which everyone's destiny is being determined.

Remember the secret mantra of the Dao: *Wuwu*! There is not even Nothing. This means one must not hold on even to the concept of Nothingness, but *be* the Emptiness. In other words, keep the mind free of thought, filled with the Love of God, but empty of ego. You will receive the *Virya*, the Virtue that makes you fearless, and enables you to hear the Word of God within the Silence. That Word is the Dao.

Glossary

AHAM AHAM

The traditional mantra from the Upanishads that indicates the state of God-consciousness. It literally means I am I.

AKANISHTA

In Tibetan Buddhism, the extremely subtle realm of consciousness which is the highest of those that contain multiple archetypal forms. Here abide the Buddhas, *Jivan Muktas*, archangels, and ascended masters, in the state ontologically prior to their final unification in the Absolute.

CHAITANYA

The Supreme Consciousness, possessing infinite intelligence, total freedom, and unlimited power.

DEVAS

Those humans who have graduated from the wisdom school that is the world, but return to enjoy life in heavenly, celestial realms, and in the first time period of Creation.

Dojo

A Japanese term for a martial arts studio. Do=Dao. Jo=a place where something is taught.

Kali Yuga

The final quadrant of time in every cycle of four *yugas*, depicted in the ancient symbol of the *swastika*. This is the period in which ego-consciousness takes over from the soul, which took over from the Holy Spirit in the previous *yuga*. The ego becomes ever more degraded as *Kali Yuga* unfolds, until it has become utterly demonic in the final years before the Great Destruction.

Koans

Riddles and questions used in the Rinzai Zen tradition as a spiritual exercise.

Kyrie eleison

God (Kyrie) have mercy (eleison), a Latin prayer.

Mahasiddhas

The greatest spiritual masters; those who have perfected all the latent powers of consciousness.

Nigredo
A term used in European alchemy, meaning blackness, and often referred to as putrefaction; the thickest tarry substance in the soul, the cause of all suffering, that must be purified and transmuted into alchemical gold.

Nirvana
The transcendent realm of eternal consciousness, in superposition with the phenomenal plane of spacetime.

Paramdhama
The highest abode of Consciousness, formless and timeless, where the Absolute Self abides in solitude beyond all manifestation.

Sahaja Samadhi
The state of a consummate yogi, abiding continuously and effortlessly in the stillness of the Absolute, even in the midst of the chaotic flux of time.

Samadhi
Consciousness abiding in its eternal nature as pure Presence, free of thought and change.

Samsara

The phenomenal world of impermanence, also known as *maya*, the realm of illusion, or of only relative reality.

Sat Chit Ananda

The first level of *Atman* consciousness, the true nature of the Self. It is unitary, but analyzed as three aspects: *Sat* means Being, or the Real; *Chit* means infinite, superconscious intelligence; *Ananda* means total, unending bliss.

Sat Yuga

In Indian philosophy, time is considered cyclical. The whole cycle is called a *kalpa*. Each *kalpa* is divided into four ages, or *yugas*. They are considered to be like the four seasons of the year, which is thought of as a microcosm of the whole of time. The first *yuga* is *Sat Yuga*. *Sat* can mean the Real, but it also refers to God, or the divine level of consciousness, in which one realizes one's consciousness is a manifestation of God, and thus one's bodily being is a god, with a lower case g. Thus, *Sat Yuga* means the Age of the gods and goddesses. It is also remembered as the Golden Age. It is followed by a Silver Age (*Treta Yuga*), a Copper Age (*Dwapur Yuga*), and an Iron Age (*Kali Yuga*), which is now ending. So we are approaching the next *Sat Yuga* now.

SATORI
A Zen term for sudden illumination.

SHIVA TATTVA
The first emanation from *Parama Shiva*, the Absolute, in which the infinite intelligence is mentalized and unfolds the implicate order of the cosmos in the most abstract symbolic form. This is what the ancient Greek philosophers called *Nous*, or the Mind of God.

SIDDHA
A yogi who has perfected consciousness by activating its latent potencies.

SIDDHI
A latent, supernormal power of human consciousness that becomes activated through the practice of the highest yoga.

SPANDA
The vibrational energy emitted by the Absolute Self, which carries information and instructions, congeals successively as a timeless ontological declension into the

Godhead, the quantum unified field, and then the phenomenal fractalized cosmos, and the explosion of the One into a myriad of particles of separated consciousness, and finally, the flux of time that creates apparent impermanence, randomness, and chaos, and then reverses the process and returns all to the Singularity.

TANDAVA

The dance of God, Lord Shiva, at the end of time. This is the act of God that destroys the world once it has been taken over by evil, and dances a new world into Being. It is referred to as a double dance. Those who are among the demonic entities perceive it as the *Rudra Tandava*, the terrible wrath of God. By those who have chosen the side of the angels, it is perceived as the *Ananda Tandava*, otherwise known by Christians as the Rapture. This has been beautifully described in a song called *The Battle Hymn of the Republic*:

> *Mine eyes have seen the glory*
> *of the coming of the Lord,*
> *He is trampling out the vintage*
> *where the grapes of wrath are stored,*
> *He hath loosed the fateful lightning*
> *of His terrible swift sword,*
> *His truth is marching on.*

Wu Wei

The Daoist term literally meaning non-action, which is more accurately defined as effortless and egoless action.

Yin and Yang

The primal twin complementary principles that permeate and replicate throughout every level of consciousness, manifesting as such pairs of opposites as transcendent and immanent, male and female, hot and cold, dark and light, dominant and recessive, etc. The shifting balance of these forces in the world are proximately responsible for the pattern of unfoldment of the explicate order.

Printed in Great Britain
by Amazon